# metropolitan
# [KNITS]

## CHIC DESIGNS
## *for* URBAN STYLE

MELISSA WEHRLE

 INTERWEAVE
interweave.com

EDITOR Erica Smith
TECHNICAL EDITOR Lori Gayle
PHOTOGRAPHER Heather Weston
ART DIRECTOR Liz Quan
COVER AND INTERIOR DESIGN Karla Baker
PHOTO STYLIST Elysha Lenkin
HAIR AND MAKEUP Julia Joseph
PRODUCTION Katherine Jackson

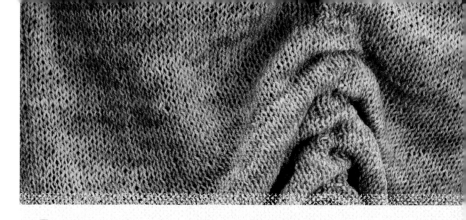

To my grandmother, who had the patience
to teach me this wonderful craft long ago

Interweave Press LLC
A division of F+W Media, Inc.
201 East Fourth Street
Loveland, CO 80537
interweave.com

Manufactured in China
by Asia Pacific Offset Ltd.

Wehrle, Melissa.
  Metropolitan knits : chic designs for urban style /
Melissa Wehrle.
    pages cm
  ISBN 978-1-59668-778-3 (pbk.)
  ISBN 978-1-62033-102-6 (PDF)
  1. Knitting--Patterns.  I. Title.
  TT825.W445 2013
  746.43'20432--dc23
                          2012048784

10 9 8 7 6 5 4 3 2 1

# contents

## chapter 1
## heart of the city

## chapter 2
## urban bohemia

## chapter 3
## city gardens

## acknowledgments

i'd like to extend a heartfelt thanks to everyone who made this book possible, especially all the wonderful people at Interweave. Thank you for all your encouragement and for believing in my work. It means more than you will ever know.

Thanks to Allison Korleski for reaching out to help me organize my ideas into an incredible proposal.

A big thank-you goes out to my editor and fellow New Yorker, Erica Smith. You helped make the daunting task of writing a book easy, and your assurances that all would go well were very comforting.

Thanks also to art director Liz Quan, for understanding my vision, making a New York photo shoot happen, and letting me tag along. Photographer Heather Weston and her crew, as well as stylist Elysha Lenkin, carried out a fantastic photo shoot.

I would like to thank Connie Chang Chinchio, Kate Gagnon Osborne, and Courtney Kelley for all your helpful advice.

Thanks to my friends Connie Chang Chinchio and Shana Wernow for lending me some of your precious time for sample knitting and Kathryn Zmrzlik for the feedback, button sewing, and keeping me well fed.

Thank you to my wonderful husband, David Bryan, who encouraged me throughout the entire book-writing process, sacrificed the precious little time we have together so I could work through many a weekend, and gave his honest opinion whenever it was requested.

Thank you to my family for all of your love, support, and passing along the crafty genes.

I also thank you, my dear knitter. Without your support, this book would have never become a reality.

# introduction

new York City is a realm of fascination and wonder for many artists, song-writers, poets, designers, filmmakers, and others throughout the world. For the last fifteen years I've lived in this wonderful city, and I've seen just about everything one could imagine—from the most fantastic art and music the world can offer to people grooming themselves on the subway. Growing up in a small farming community in southern New Jersey, I didn't know at first what I was getting myself into. It took me a while to adjust, but now I couldn't imagine my life without New York; the city has helped shaped me into the person I am today. I have come to embrace, and feel I am ever embraced by, all of the sights and sounds of this city. New York is the muse that inspires and carries me through my days as both a designer and an artist.

New York is a great place to live, work, and play. Everything is right at your fingertips twenty-four hours a day, seven days a week. (Not to mention we have more yarn stores than I can count on the fingers of both hands!) Cultures, ideas, and creativity blend seamlessly into source of never-ending inspiration.

For this book, I tried to capture the heart and soul of the city, designing knitwear that will take you through the many and varied experiences the city affords to residents and visitors alike. In these pages, you will find just the right sweater for the occasion: From walking the busy thoroughfares of Manhattan, to relaxing at your favorite coffee shop on the weekend, to enjoying the many peaceful green spaces and parks throughout the city. While the city often seems to be always in a constant state of change and upheaval, I hope that these designs will be timeless, well-worn additions to your wardrobe that will last through the never-ending, sometimes fickle, changes in trends and fashion. These pieces will show off your knitting skills and maybe even teach you some new skills along the way.

Great care was given to the selection of yarn for each design. A wide range of yarn weights, price ranges, and materials were used to suit everyone's taste. I used yarns that I personally love for one reason or another, carefully matching the yarn properties of drape, shine, and feel to each individual design. However, yarn weights are also provided should you wish to substitute with a yarn of your liking.

It is my sincere intention that within these pages you will find designs that not only inspire you but that will also become cherished additions to your sweater collection. Also, I hope to bring a little bit of New York style home to you, wherever you may live.

## chapter 1

# HEART OF THE CITY

the heart of the city is all about kinetic energy: the entangled traffic and underground trains; the constant hum of international business and trade; the bright theater district and coy street performers; the frenetic tourists at sophisticated shops, fashion week, concerts, and museums. And yet in the midst of all of this chaos, there is calm.

The steady hum of the intricate parts makes the city a center of limitless creativity. The city is a living, breathing organism, changing, growing, and moving. As the human heart is the life force—the energizing organ that sustains us and gives us life—so, too, is the heart of the city.

This chapter is about movement—of light, sound, touch, and sight. In this section, the designs are slightly more sophisticated in silhouette and material, suited to any "uptown girl." But don't let that limit you; these pieces feel just as much at home in a more casual setting as well. The designs that follow have an abundance of little details to discover, just as one might stumble upon that great little old-fashioned bakery nestled in between towering glass skyscrapers.

# opera house MITTS

### FINISHED SIZE
6" (15 cm) hand circumference (will stretch to about 7½" [19 cm]) and 10½" (26.5 cm) long.

### YARN
Sportweight (#2 Fine).

**SHOWN HERE:** Bijou Basin Ranch *Bijou Spun Lhasa Wilderness* (75% yak, 25% bamboo; 180 yd [165 m]/56 g): #01 natural brown, 1 skein.

### NEEDLES
**MITTS**—size U.S. 3 (3.25 mm): double-pointed needles (dpn).

**RIBBING**—size U.S. 2 (2.75 mm): dpn.

*Adjust needle sizes, if necessary, to obtain the correct gauge.*

### NOTIONS
Markers (m); stitch holder or waste yarn; removable stitch markers or safety pins; tapestry needle; sewing needle and matching thread; two ½" (13 mm) shank buttons.

### GAUGE
27 sts and 48 rnds in Mock Honeycomb patt on larger needles.

You may or may not have musical talent, but either way, you certainly can make yourself a smart pair of mitts worthy of wearing to the performance. The mock honeycomb pattern is very simple to memorize and moves along rather quickly in the round. This is the perfect project for that luxury skein of yarn you've been holding on to for a special occasion.

# stitch guide

## K1, P1 RIB IN THE ROUND
*(even number of sts)*

ALL RNDS: *K1, p1; rep from *.

Rep this rnd for patt.

## K1, P1 RIB IN ROWS
*(odd number of sts)*

ROW 1: (RS) K1, *p1, k1; rep from *.

ROW 2: (WS) P1, *k1, p1; rep from *.

Rep Rows 1 and 2 for patt.

## MOCK HONEYCOMB
*(multiple of 4 sts)*

Slip all sts purlwise (pwise).

RNDS 1, 3, 5: Knit.

RNDS 2 and 4: *Sl 3 sts wyf, k1, rep from *.

RND 6: K1, *insert right needle tip under the 2 loose slipped strands from Rnds 2 and 4 and into the next st, knit the next st tog with the strands, k3; rep from *, to last 2 sts, k2.

RND 7: Knit.

RNDS 8 AND 10: K2, *sl 3 sts wyf, k1; rep from * to last 2 sts, sl last 2 sts wyf, sl end-of-rnd marker (m), sl next st wyf (the first st of the foll rnd).

RNDS 9 AND 11: Knit to end of rnd (first st was slipped at end of previous rnd).

RND 12: K3, *insert right needle tip under the 2 loose slipped strands from Rnds 8 and 10 and into the next st, knit next st tog with the strands, k3; rep from * to last st, insert right needle tip under 2 loose strands from Rnds 8 and 10 and into the last st, knit last st tog with the strands.

Rep Rnds 1–12 for patt.

# note

⊖ Both mitts are worked the same and can be worn on either hand.

# mitts

## Cuff and Lower Hand

With smaller dpn, CO 46 sts. Place marker (pm) and join in the round, being careful not to twist sts. Work in k1, p1 rib in the rnd (see Stitch Guide) until cuff measures 1½" (3.8 cm).

Change to larger dpn. Work Rnd 1 of mock honeycomb patt (see Stitch Guide) and *at the same time* dec 6 sts evenly spaced—40 sts rem.

Continue in mock honeycomb patt until 66 patt rnds have been completed, ending with Rnd 6 of patt—piece measures 7" (18 cm) from CO.

## Thumb Gusset

**note:** *The gusset sts between the thumb markers are worked in St st; maintain the mock honeycomb patt as well as possible on each side of the gusset.*

SETUP RND (RND 7 OF PATT): K21, pm, k1, pm, k18—1 gusset st between m.

INC RND: Work in patt to first gusset m, sl m, M1 (see Techniques), knit to next gusset m, M1, sl m, work in patt to end—2 gusset sts inc'd.

Work 1 rnd even in patt. Cont in patt, rep the shaping of the last 2 rnds 7 more times—17 gusset sts between m, 56 sts total.

NEXT RND: Work in patt to first gusset m, remove m, place 17 sts on holder, remove m, CO 1 st over gap using the backward-loop method (see Techniques), work in patt to end—40 sts.

## Upper Hand

Cont in established patt until Rnds 1–12 of mock honeycomb patt have been worked a total of 8 times, then work Rnds 1–6 once more—102 patt rnds total; piece measures 10" (25.5 cm) from CO.

Change to smaller needles. Knit 1 rnd, inc 6 sts evenly spaced—46 sts.

Work in k1, p1 rib in the rnd for 4 rnds—piece measures 10½" (26.5 cm) from CO. BO all sts using the tubular k1, p1 rib BO method (see Techniques).

# finishing

## Thumb

Place 17 held thumb sts on larger dpn and distribute as evenly as possible on 3 dpn. Join yarn to beg of sts with RS facing.

NEXT RND: K17, pick up and knit 1 st from base of st CO across thumb gap—18 sts.

Knit 1 rnd. Work k1, p1 rib in the rnd for 4 rnds. BO all sts using the tubular k1, p1 rib BO method. Work second thumb in the same manner.

## Button Tabs (make 2)

With 2 smaller dpn, CO 9 sts. Working back and forth in rows, work in St st for 4 rows. Change to k1, p1 rib in rows (see Stitch Guide) and work in rib patt until tab measures 2¼" (5.5 cm) from CO, ending with a WS row.

DEC ROW: (RS) Ssk, work in patt to last 2 sts, k2tog—2 sts dec'd.

Cont in patt, rep the dec row on the next 2 RS rows, then work 1 WS row even—3 sts rem.

NEXT ROW: (RS) Sl 2 sts as if to k2tog, k1, pass 2 slipped sts over—1 st rem.

Cut yarn and fasten off last st. Work a second tab in the same manner.

Block mitts and button tabs. Weave in ends.

Try mitts on and use removable markers or safety pins to position button tabs at CO edges of mitts where they look best to you. For the mitts shown, the tabs are attached to the pinky side of each mitt, opposite the thumb gussets. Fold the St st section of each tab around the CO edge of the mitt so only the ribbed portion of the tab shows on the RS of the mitt. Using sewing needle and thread, sew CO edge of each tab invisibly to WS of mitt. Sew a button about 1" (2.5 cm) from the pointed end of each tab as shown, sewing through both layers of the tab and mitt.

# uptown SCARF

### FINISHED SIZE

About 6"–9½" (15–24 cm) wide and 73"
(185.5 cm) long.

### YARN

Sportweight (#2 Fine).

**SHOWN HERE:** Rowan *Kidsilk Haze* (70%
super kid mohair, 30% silk; 229 yd
[210 m]/25 g): #605 smoke, 2 balls.

### NEEDLES

Size U.S. 7 (4.5 mm): straight.

*Adjust needle size, if necessary, to obtain
the correct gauge.*

### NOTIONS

Tapestry needle.

### GAUGE

21 sts and 28 rows = 4" (10 cm) in St st,
blocked.

25 sts in pin tucks measure about 6"
(15 cm) wide, blocked.

20 rows (1 patt rep) of pin tuck stripe
measure about 2¾" (7 cm) high, blocked.

Kidsilk Haze is one of my all-time favorite yarns. It's so
versatile and makes the most beautiful soft fabric. For this
scarf, I used a needle size at the large end of the suggested
range to achieve a very open fabric and then narrowed the
width for the pin tucks. This scarf is the perfect accessory
for the first chilly days of fall; it fits right in with the gray
streets and keeps the breeze at bay!

## stitch guide

### PIN TUCK STRIPE
*(even number of sts)*

ROW 1: (RS) *K2tog; rep from * to end of row—sts have dec'd to one-half the starting number.

ROWS 2–5: Work in St st for 4 rows, ending with a RS row.

ROW 6: (WS, tucking row) *Identify the st in Row 2 that is 4 rows below the next st on the left needle, insert the right needle tip into the purl bump of this st and lift it onto the left needle, then work the lifted st and the next st on the needle tog loosely as p2tog; rep from * to end of row.

ROW 7: *K1f&b (see Techniques); rep from * to end of row—sts have increased to the starting number again.

ROWS 8–20: Work in St st for 13 rows, beg and ending with a WS row.

Rep Rows 1–20 for patt.

## note

⊖ The stitch count of the pin tuck stripe pattern does not remain constant throughout. The number of stitches is decreased by half for the tucked section in Rows 1–6 and then increases to the original stitch count again in Row 7.

## scarf

CO 50 sts. Work in St st for 27 rows, ending with a WS row—piece measures about 3¾" (9.5 cm) from CO. Work Rows 1–20 of pin tuck stripe (see Stitch Guide) 23 times, then work Rows 1–7 once more, ending with a RS row—50 sts; 24 pin tucks completed. Work in St st for 26 rows, beg and ending with a WS row. BO all sts loosely.

## finishing

Weave in all ends. Block to measurements, allowing selvedges to roll gently to WS.

# museum SWEATER

## FINISHED SIZE

31 (34½, 37, 39, 42, 45, 49)" (78.5 [87.5, 94, 99, 106.5, 114.5, 124.5] cm) bust circumference. Pullover shown measures 31" (78.5 cm).

## YARN

DK Weight (#3 Light).

**SHOWN HERE:** Blue Sky Alpacas *Alpaca Silk* (50% alpaca, 50% silk; 146 yd [133 m]/50 g): #148 peridot, 9 (9, 10, 11, 11, 12, 14) skeins.

## NEEDLES

**BODY AND SLEEVES**—size U.S. 5 (3.75 mm): 16" and 24" (40.5 and 61 cm) circular (cir) needles.

*Adjust needle size, if necessary, to obtain the correct gauge.*

## NOTIONS

Marker (m); removable stitch markers; stitch holders; tapestry needle.

## GAUGE

23 sts and 28 rows = 4" (10 cm) in pattern from Body and Sleeve charts.

A beautiful shiny yarn meets modern simplicity in this fitted, textured lace sweater. Spend an afternoon visiting the hallowed museums of New York feeling both posh and comfortable! The arched shape of the lace pattern reminds me of the windows you might find in an exhibit of medieval art. The stitch pattern will stretch slightly when worn, so I suggest choosing a finished size with negative ease, about 2" (5 cm) smaller than your chest measurement.

# stitch guide

## TWISTED RIB IN ROWS
### (even number of sts)

ROWS 1 (RS) AND 2 (WS): *K1tbl, p1; rep from * to end.

Rep Rows 1 and 2 for patt.

note: *Each stitch column will contain a twisted stitch every other row.*

## TWISTED RIB IN ROWS
### (odd number of sts)

ROW 1: (RS) K1tbl, *p1, k1tbl; rep from * to end.

ROW 2: (WS) P1, *k1tbl, p1; rep from * to end.

Rep Rows 1 and 2 for patt.

note: *Each stitch column will contain a twisted stitch every other row.*

## TWISTED RIB IN ROUNDS
### (even number of sts)

ALL RNDS: *K1tbl, p1; rep from * to end.

Rep this rnd for patt.

note: *Only the knit columns on the RS of the cowl will contain twisted stitches, and they will be twisted every round.*

## RT3 (RIGHT TWIST 3)
Skipping the first 2 sts on left needle, knit into the third st, then knit into the second st, then knit into the first st, and slip all 3 sts from the needle together.

# notes

⊖ The gauge swatch for this project is important for two reasons. First, the yarn shown has a smooth, silky surface with a lot of drape, so it's important to make a large enough swatch to determine how the fabric will behave. Second, the lace pattern has a "spring" to it and may contract after blocking when it is released from the pins. I have three suggestions for success: Make a gauge swatch at least 6" (15 cm) square or larger, wet block your swatch and allow it to dry completely, and, finally, let the swatch relax for a day or two after you remove the pins before you measure its gauge. Trust me: this extra effort will be well worth your time and energy.

⊖ To make seaming easier, work the first and last stitches of each row in stockinette.

⊖ When working the charted lace patterns, if your size does not have enough stitches outside the marked pattern repeat to work an entire 3-stitch twist or a decrease with its companion yarnover, work the stitches in stockinette instead.

⊖ To keep track of the lace patterns during shaping, place removable stitch markers at the beginning of the first full repeat and at the end of the last full repeat. When decreasing, work the stitches of any partial repeats outside the markers in stockinette, then move the markers inward as necessary. When increasing, work the new stitches of any partial repeats outside the markers in stockinette until there are enough stitches to work them into the established lace pattern, then move the markers outward as necessary.

# back

Using longer cir needle and the tubular CO method (see Techniques), CO 96 (104, 114, 120, 130, 140, 152) sts. Work in twisted rib patt in rows (see Stitch Guide) until piece measures 1½" (3.8 cm), ending with a WS row.

DEC ROW: (RS) K5 (11, 8, 5, 8, 5, 11) [k2tog, k5 (6, 6, 7, 6, 6, 6)] 12 (10, 12, 12, 14, 16, 16) times, k2tog, k5 (11, 8, 5, 8, 5, 11)—83 (93, 101, 107, 115, 123, 135) sts.

Purl 1 WS row.

NEXT ROW: (RS) K1 (selvedge st; see Notes), beg and ending where indicated for your size, work Row 1 of Body chart over center 81 (91, 99, 105, 113, 121, 133) sts, k1 (selvedge st).

Keeping selvedge sts at each side in St st, cont in established patt until piece measures 2½" (6.5 cm) from CO, ending with a WS row.

## Shape Waist

DEC ROW: (RS) K1, ssk, work in patt to last 3 sts, k2tog, k1—2 sts dec'd.

Cont in patt (see Notes), rep the dec row every 10 (10, 10, 10, 12, 12, 12) rows 2 (2, 1, 1, 3, 2, 2) more time(s), then every 12 (12, 12, 12, 0, 14, 14) rows 1 (1, 2, 2, 0, 1, 1) time(s)—75 (85, 93, 99, 107, 115, 127) sts rem.

Work even for 7 rows after the last dec row, beg and ending with a WS row—piece measures 8¼, (8¼, 8½, 8½, 8¾, 9, 9)" (21 [21, 21.5, 21.5, 22, 23, 23] cm) from CO.

INC ROW: (RS) K1, M1 (see Techniques), work in patt to last st, M1, k1—2 sts inc'd.

Cont in patt, rep the inc row every 6 rows 6 (6, 5, 5, 4, 3, 3) more times, then every 0 (0, 8, 8, 8, 8, 8) rows 0 (0, 1, 1, 2, 3, 3) time(s), working new sts into patt (see Notes)—89 (99, 107, 113, 121, 129, 141) sts.

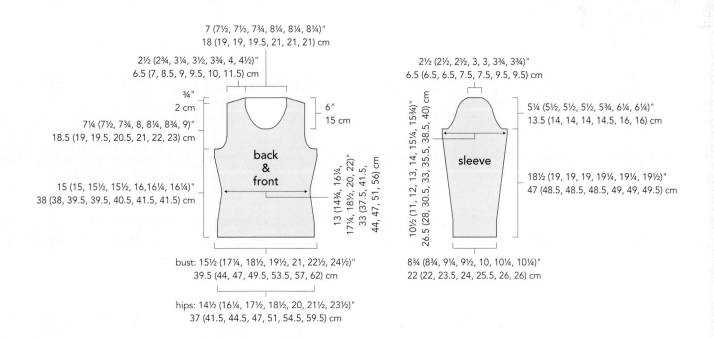

7 (7½, 7½, 7¾, 8¼, 8¼, 8¼)"
18 (19, 19, 19.5, 21, 21, 21) cm

2½ (2¾, 3¼, 3½, 3¾, 4, 4½)"
6.5 (7, 8.5, 9, 9.5, 10, 11.5) cm

¾"
2 cm

7¼ (7½, 7¾, 8, 8¼, 8¾, 9)"
18.5 (19, 19.5, 20.5, 21, 22, 23) cm

6"
15 cm

15 (15, 15½, 15½, 16, 16¼, 16¼)"
38 (38, 39.5, 39.5, 40.5, 41.5, 41.5) cm

back & front

13 (14¾, 16¼, 17¼, 18½, 20, 22)"
33 (37.5, 41.5, 44, 47, 51, 56) cm

bust: 15½ (17¼, 18½, 19½, 21, 22½, 24½)"
39.5 (44, 47, 49.5, 53.5, 57, 62) cm

hips: 14½ (16¼, 17½, 18½, 20, 21½, 23½)"
37 (41.5, 44.5, 47, 51, 54.5, 59.5) cm

2½ (2½, 2½, 3, 3, 3¾, 3¾)"
6.5 (6.5, 6.5, 7.5, 7.5, 9.5, 9.5) cm

5¼ (5½, 5½, 5½, 5¾, 6¼, 6¼)"
13.5 (14, 14, 14, 14.5, 16, 16) cm

sleeve

10½ (11, 12, 13, 14, 15¼, 15¾)"
26.5 (28, 30.5, 33, 35.5, 38.5, 40) cm

18½ (19, 19, 19, 19¼, 19¼, 19½)"
47 (48.5, 48.5, 48.5, 49, 49, 49.5) cm

8¾ (8¾, 9¼, 9½, 10, 10¼, 10¼)"
22 (22, 23.5, 24, 25.5, 26, 26) cm

Work even in patt until piece measures 15 (15, 15½, 15½, 16, 16¼, 16¼)" (38 [38, 39.5, 39.5, 40.5, 41.5, 41.5] cm) from CO, ending with a WS row.

## Shape Armholes

BO 5 (6, 7, 7, 8, 9, 10) sts at beg of next 2 rows—79 (87, 93, 99, 105, 111, 121) sts.

NEXT ROW: (RS) K1, ssk, work in patt to last 3 sts, k2tog, k1—2 sts dec'd.

NEXT ROW: (WS) P1, p2tog, work in patt to last 3 sts, ssp (see Techniques), p1—2 sts dec'd.

Rep the last 2 rows 1 (2, 2, 2, 2, 3, 4) more time(s), then work the RS dec row 0 (0, 0, 1, 1, 1, 1) more time—71 (75, 81, 85, 91, 93, 99) sts rem.

Cont in patt until armholes measure 7¼ (7½, 7¾, 8, 8¼, 8¾, 9)" (18.5 [19, 19.5, 20.5, 21, 22, 23] cm), ending with a WS row.

## Shape Back Neck and Shoulders

NEXT ROW: (RS) BO 5 (5, 6, 7, 7, 8, 9) sts, work in patt until there are 12 (13, 15, 15, 17, 17, 19) sts on right needle after BO, place rem 54 (57, 60, 63, 67, 68, 71) sts on holder; 12 (13, 15, 15, 17, 17, 19) right back shoulder sts rem on needle.

Cont as foll:

## Right Back Shoulder

NEXT ROW: (WS) P2tog at neck edge, work in patt to end—11 (12, 14, 14, 16, 16, 18) sts.

NEXT ROW: (RS) BO 5 (5, 6, 7, 7, 8, 9) sts, work in patt to last 2 sts, ssk—5 (6, 7, 6, 8, 7, 8) sts rem.

NEXT ROW: Work 1 WS row even.

BO all sts with RS facing.

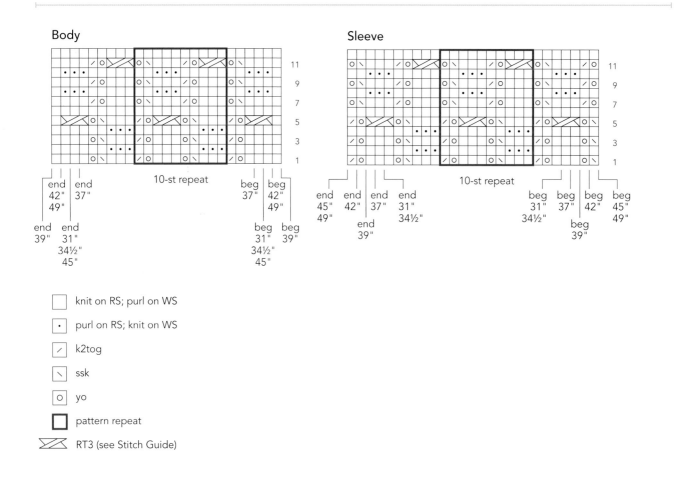

**Body**

10-st repeat

end 42" 49"  end 37"  beg 37"  beg 42" 49"

end 39"  end 31" 34½" 45"  beg 31" 34½" 45"  beg 39"

**Sleeve**

10-st repeat

end 45" 49"  end 42"  end 37" 34½"  end 31"  beg 31" 34½"  beg 37"  beg 42"  beg 45" 49"

end 39"  beg 39"

- ☐ knit on RS; purl on WS
- • purl on RS; knit on WS
- ╱ k2tog
- ╲ ssk
- ○ yo
- ☐ pattern repeat
- ⧄ RT3 (see Stitch Guide)

## Left Back Shoulder

Return 54 (57, 60, 63, 67, 68, 71) held sts to needle and rejoin yarn with RS facing.

**NEXT ROW:** (RS) BO 37 (39, 39, 41, 43, 43, 43) back neck sts, work in patt to end—17 (18, 21, 22, 24, 25, 28) sts rem.

**NEXT ROW:** (WS) BO 5 (5, 6, 7, 7, 8, 9) sts, work in patt to last 2 sts, ssp at neck edge—11 (12, 14, 14, 16, 16, 18) sts.

**NEXT ROW:** K2tog, work in patt to end—10 (11, 13, 13, 15, 15, 17) sts.

**NEXT ROW:** BO 5 (5, 6, 7, 7, 8, 9) sts, work in patt to end—5 (6, 7, 6, 8, 7, 8) sts.

BO all sts with RS facing.

# front

Work as for back until armhole shaping has been completed—71 (75, 81, 85, 91, 93, 99) sts. Cont even in patt until armholes measure 2 (2¼, 2½, 2¾, 3, 3½, 3¾)" (5 [5.5, 6.5, 7, 7.5, 9, 9.5] cm), ending with a WS row.

## Shape Front Neck

Place a removable m on each side of the center 3 (3, 3, 5, 5, 7, 7) sts—34 (36, 39, 40, 43, 43, 46) sts each side of marked sts.

**NEXT ROW:** (RS) Removing m as you come to them, work in patt to marked sts, join a second ball of yarn and BO center 3 (3, 3, 3, 5, 5, 7, 7) sts, work in patt to end—34 (36, 39, 40, 43, 43, 46) sts each side.

Working each side separately, dec 1 st at each neck edge every row 11 times, then every RS row (i.e., every other row) 8 (9, 9, 9, 10, 9, 9) times—15 (16, 19, 20, 22, 23, 26) sts rem at each side.

Cont in patt until armholes measure 7¼ (7½, 7¾, 8, 8¼, 8¾, 9)" (18.5 [19, 19.5, 20.5, 21, 22, 23] cm), ending with a WS row.

## Shape Shoulders

Cont to work each side separately, at each armhole edge BO 5 (5, 6, 7, 7, 8, 9) sts 2 times, then BO 5 (6, 7, 6, 8, 7, 8) sts once—no sts rem.

## sleeves

Using longer cir and the tubular CO method, CO 51 (51, 53, 55, 57, 59, 59) sts. Work twisted rib patt in rows until piece measures 1½" (3.8 cm), ending with a WS row.

NEXT ROW: (RS) K1 (selvedge st), beg and ending where indicated for your size, work Row 1 of Sleeve chart over center 49 (49, 51, 53, 55, 57, 57) sts, k1 (selvedge st).

Keeping selvedges sts at each side in St st, cont in established patt until piece measures 3" (7.5 cm) from CO, ending with a WS row.

INC ROW: (RS) K1, M1, work in patt to last st, M1, k1—2 sts inc'd.

Cont in patt, rep the inc row every 26 (20, 14, 10, 8, 8, 6) rows 4 (3, 4, 2, 2, 12, 6) more times, then every 0 (22, 16, 12, 10, 10, 8) rows 0 (2, 3, 7, 9, 1, 9) time(s), working new sts into patt—61 (63, 69, 75, 81, 87, 91) sts.

Work even in patt until piece measures 18½ (19, 19, 19, 19¼, 19¼, 19½)" (47 [48.5, 48.5, 48.5, 49, 49, 49.5] cm) from CO, ending with a WS row.

### Shape Sleeve Cap

BO 5 (6, 7, 7, 8, 9, 10) sts at beg of next 2 rows—51 (51, 55, 61, 65, 69, 71) sts rem.

DEC ROW: (RS) K1, ssk, work in patt to last 3 sts, k2tog, k1—2 sts dec'd.

Rep the dec row every RS row 4 (2, 3, 4, 5, 4, 4) times, then every 4 rows (i.e., every other RS row) 4 (5, 4, 2, 2, 4, 4) times, then every RS row 1 (2, 2, 5, 4, 3, 2) time(s)—31 (31, 35, 37, 41, 45, 49) sts.

NEXT ROW: (WS) P1, p2tog, work in patt to last 3 sts, ssp, p1—2 sts dec'd.

NEXT ROW: (RS) K1, ssk, work in patt to last 3 sts, k2tog, k1—2 sts dec'd.

Rep the last 2 rows 1 (1, 2, 2, 3, 3, 4) more time(s), then work the WS dec row 1 more time—21 (21, 21, 23, 23, 27, 27) sts rem. BO 3 sts at the beg of next 2 rows—15 (15, 15, 17, 17, 21, 21) sts. BO all sts.

## finishing

Block pieces to measurements. With yarn threaded on a tapestry needle, sew shoulder seams. Sew sleeves into armholes. Sew sleeve and side seams.

### Cowl

**note:** *The RS of the cowl corresponds to the WS of the sweater so the RS of the cowl will show when it is folded back, turtleneck-fashion.*

With shorter cir needle and RS facing, pick up and knit 200 (204, 204, 206, 208, 208, 208) sts around neck opening. Turn sweater inside out and reverse the direction of the knitting; the RS of the cowl and the WS of the sweater will be facing you.

NEXT RND: Work twisted rib in the rnd (see Stitch Guide) to end, then pm and join for working in the rnd.

Cont in twisted rib patt until piece measures 10 (10, 10, 10½, 10½, 11, 11)" (25.5 [25.5, 25.5, 26.5, 26.5, 28, 28] cm) from pickup rnd.

NEXT 2 RNDS: *K1tbl, sl 1 purlwise with yarn in back; rep from * to end of rnd.

BO all sts using the tubular k1, p1 rib BO method (see Techniques).

Weave in all loose ends. Block cowl, if desired.

# le cirque
## COWLNECK SWEATER

**FINISHED SIZE**
30½ (34¼, 37¾, 42¼, 45¾)" (77.5 [87, 96, 107.5, 116] cm) bust circumference. Pullover shown measures 34¼" (87 cm).

**YARN**
Sportweight (#2 Fine).

**SHOWN HERE:** The Fibre Company *Road to China Light* (65% baby alpaca, 15% silk, 10% cashmere, 10% camel; 159 yd [145 m]/50 g): garnet, 7 (8, 9, 10, 11) skeins.

**NEEDLES**
**BODY AND SLEEVES**—size U.S. 6 (4 mm): 24" (61 cm) circular (cir) needle.

**EDGINGS**—size U.S. 5 (3.75 mm): 24" (61 cm) cir needle.

*Adjust needle sizes, if necessary, to obtain the correct gauge.*

**NOTIONS**
Markers (m); removable markers; stitch holders; tapestry needle; sewing needle and matching thread; three ⅝" (1.5 cm) buttons.

**GAUGE**
22 sts and 28 rows/rnds = 4" (10 cm) in textured stripe patt on larger needle.

A simple textured stripe adds interest to a drapey, modern drop-shoulder pullover. Using a sportweight yarn knit at a DK gauge allows the cowl neck to drape just right. Knit in the round up to the armholes, the sweater has very little to seam. I chose to work my sleeves flat, because that is how I like to work, but they could easily be converted into the round by taking out the two selvedge stitches that would be used for the seam. This sweater evokes the polish of its namesake haute restaurant, with just enough softness around the edges.

## stitch guide

### TEXTURED STRIPE IN ROUNDS
*(odd number of sts)*

RNDS 1–13: Knit.

RND 14: Purl.

RND 15: *K2tog, yo; rep from * to last st, k1.

RND 16: Purl.

Rep Rnds 1–16 for patt.

### TEXTURED STRIPE IN ROWS
*(odd number of sts)*

ROW 1 (RS): Knit.

ROW 2: (WS) Purl.

ROWS 3–12: Rep Rows 1 and 2 five more times.

ROWS 13–14: Knit.

ROW 15: *K2tog, yo; rep from * to last st, k1.

ROW 16: Knit.

Rep Rows 1–16 for patt.

## notes

⊖ The body is worked in the round to just below the armholes, then divided for working the front and back separately. The sleeves are worked in rows.

⊖ During shaping, if there are not enough stitches to work a yarnover with its companion k2tog decrease, work the remaining stitch as k1 to avoid throwing off the stitch count.

⊖ Why a faux button placket on the back? When functionality isn't important, a faux button placket is a nice added detail. A faux placket avoids the extra work of splitting the back into separate halves and having to finish the placket, and it can never pull or gap the way a real button placket can.

## body

### Hem

With smaller cir needle, CO 164 (184, 204, 228, 248) sts. Pm and join in the rnd, being careful not to twist sts. Knit 6 rnds. Purl 1 rnd for fold line. Knit 6 rnds—piece measures about ¾" (2 cm) from fold line. Change to larger cir needle.

SETUP RND: Work Rnd 1 of textured stripe in rnds (see Stitch Guide) over 81 (91, 101, 113, 123) front sts, p1 for "seam" st, pm for left side, work Rnd 1 of textured stripe in rnds over 81 (91, 101, 113, 123) back sts, p1 for "seam" st.

Purling "seam" sts every rnd, work in patt until piece measures 2½" (6.5 cm) from fold line.

### Shape Waist

DEC RND: *Ssk, work to 3 sts before m, k2tog, p1, slip marker (sl m); rep from * once more— 4 sts dec'd; 2 sts each from front and back.

Cont in patt, rep the dec rnd every 12 rnds 2 (2, 2, 1, 1) more time(s), then every 14 rnds 1 (1, 1, 2, 2) time(s)—148 (168, 188, 212, 232) sts rem; 74 (84, 94, 106, 116) sts each for front and back; piece measures 8 (8, 8, 8¼, 8¼)" (20.5 [20.5, 20.5, 21, 21] cm) from fold line. Work even in patt for 1" (2.5 cm).

INC RND: *K1, M1 (see Techniques), work to 2 sts before m, M1, k1, p1; rep from * once more— 4 sts inc'd; 2 sts each for front and back.

Cont in patt, rep the inc rnd every 8 rnds 3 (3, 1, 1, 1) more times, then every 10 rnds 1 (1, 3, 3, 3) time(s)—168 (188, 208, 232, 252) sts; 84 (94, 104, 116, 126) sts each for front and back. Work even if necessary until piece measures 14 (14, 14½, 14¾, 14¾)" (35.5 [35.5, 37, 37.5 37.5] cm) from fold line, ending with an even-numbered patt rnd, and ending last rnd 1 st before end-of-rnd marker.

DIVIDING RND: BO 1 st (last st of previous rnd), work in patt until there are 83 (93, 103, 115, 125) sts on right needle after BO gap, BO 1 st, work in patt to end—83 (93, 103, 115, 125) sts each for front and back. Place front sts on holder.

## back

Change to working the textured stripe in rows (see Stitch Guide), beginning with the WS even-numbered row that follows the odd-numbered rnd just completed. For example, if you worked the dividing round on Rnd 5 of the pattern, continue the pattern in rows beginning with Row 6.

NEXT ROW: (WS) Work even in patt.

INC ROW: (RS) K1, M1, work in patt to last st, M1, k1—2 sts inc'd.

Cont in patt, rep the shaping of the last 2 rows 3 more times, working new sts into patt—91 (101, 111, 123, 133) sts.

NEXT 2 ROWS: Work in patt to end, use the backward loop method (see Techniques) to CO 4 sts for base of armholes—99 (109, 119, 131, 141) sts; back measures 1½" (3.8 cm) from dividing round.

Work even in patt until back measures 3 (3, 3½, 4¼, 4¾)" (7.5 [7.5, 9, 11, 12] cm) from dividing round, ending with a WS row.

### Faux Placket

NEXT ROW: (RS) Work 45 (50, 55, 61, 66) sts in patt, pm, work center 9 sts as [p1, k1] 4 times, p1, pm, work 45 (50, 55, 61, 66) sts in patt.

Working 9 marked center back sts in rib patt as they appear (knit the knits and purl the purls), work rem sts in established patt (see Notes) until

back measures 7 (7, 7½, 8¼, 8¾)" (18 [18, 19, 21, 22] cm) from dividing round and 5½ (5½, 6, 6¾, 7¼)" (14 [14, 15, 17, 18.5] cm) from sts CO at each side for armholes, ending with a WS row.

## Shape Shoulders

Cont faux placket and main patt as established, BO 4 (5, 5, 6, 7) sts at beg of next 8 rows—67 (69, 79, 83, 85) sts rem.

### Right back shoulder

NEXT ROW: (RS) BO 4 (5, 5, 7, 7) sts, work in patt until there are 11 (11, 16, 16, 17) sts on right needle after BO, place next 52 (53, 58, 60, 61) sts on holder—11 (11, 16, 16, 17) right shoulder sts rem on needle.

NEXT ROW: (WS) P2tog at neck edge, work in patt to end—10 (10, 15, 15, 16) sts.

NEXT ROW: BO 5 (5, 7, 7, 7) sts, work in patt to last 2 sts, k2tog—4 (4, 7, 7, 8) sts.

NEXT ROW: Work even in patt.

BO all sts with RS facing.

### Left back shoulder

Return 52 (53, 58, 60, 61) held sts to needle and rejoin yarn with RS facing.

NEXT ROW: (RS) BO 37 center back sts, work in patt to end—15 (16, 21, 23, 24) sts rem.

NEXT ROW: (WS) BO 4 (5, 5, 7, 7) sts, work in patt to last 2 sts, ssp (see Techniques) at neck edge—10 (10, 15, 15, 16) sts.

NEXT ROW: Ssk at neck edge, work in patt to end—9 (9, 14, 14, 15) sts.

NEXT ROW: BO 5 (5, 7, 7, 7) sts, work in patt to end—4 (4, 7, 7, 8) sts.

BO all sts with RS facing.

# front

Return 83 (93, 103, 115, 125) held front sts to larger cir needle and rejoin yarn with WS facing. Change to working the textured stripe in rows beginning with the same WS row as the back.

NEXT ROW: (WS) Work even in patt.

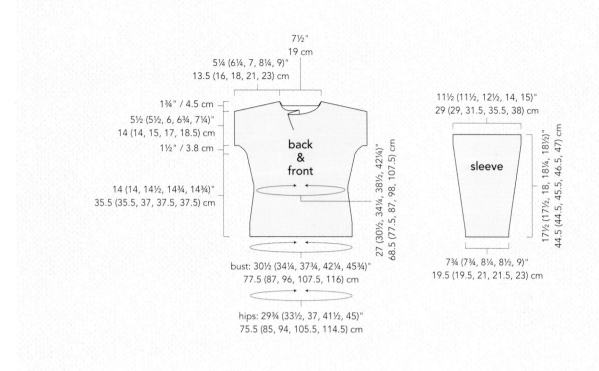

**7½"**
**19 cm**

5¼ (6¼, 7, 8¼, 9)"
13.5 (16, 18, 21, 23) cm

11½ (11½, 12½, 14, 15)"
29 (29, 31.5, 35.5, 38) cm

1¾" / 4.5 cm

5½ (5½, 6, 6¾, 7¼)"
14 (14, 15, 17, 18.5) cm

1½" / 3.8 cm

back
&
front

sleeve

14 (14, 14½, 14¾, 14¾)"
35.5 (35.5, 37, 37.5, 37.5) cm

27 (30½, 34¼, 38½, 42¼)"
68.5 (77.5, 87, 98, 107.5) cm

17½ (17½, 18, 18¼, 18½)"
44.5 (44.5, 45.5, 46.5, 47) cm

bust: 30½ (34¼, 37¾, 42¼, 45¾)"
77.5 (87, 96, 107.5, 116) cm

7¾ (7¾, 8¼, 8½, 9)"
19.5 (19.5, 21, 21.5, 23) cm

hips: 29¾ (33½, 37, 41½, 45)"
75.5 (85, 94, 105.5, 114.5) cm

**INC ROW:** (RS) K1, M1, work in patt to last st, M1, k1—2 sts inc'd.

Cont in patt, rep the shaping of the last 2 rows 3 more times, working new sts into patt—91 (101, 111, 123, 133) sts.

**NEXT 2 ROWS:** Work in patt to end, use the backward-loop method to CO 4 sts for base of armholes—99 (109, 119, 131, 141) sts; front measures 1½" (3.8 cm) from dividing round.

## Shape Cowl

**note:** *As you work the cowl shaping, if a cowl increase row happens to fall on Row 15 of the textured stripe pattern, you can increase 1 stitch invisibly in pattern by substituting [k1, yo] for [k2tog, yo] at each point where an increase is needed, instead of working an M1 increase.*

**SETUP ROW:** (WS) Work 49 (54, 59, 65, 70) sts in patt, pm, p1, pm work 49 (54, 59, 65, 70) sts in patt.

**ROW 1:** (RS) Work in patt to first cowl m, M1, sl m, k1, sl m, M1, work in patt to end—2 sts inc.

**ROW 2:** Work even in patt.

**ROW 3:** Work in patt to 2 sts before center st, M1, place removable m, k2, sl m, k1 (center st), sl m, k2, place removable m, M1, work in patt to end—2 sts inc'd.

**ROW 4:** Work even in patt.

**ROW 5:** Slipping removable m as you come to them, work in patt to marked center st, M1, sl m, k1, sl m, M1, work in patt to end—2 sts inc'd.

**ROW 6:** Work even in patt.

**ROW 7:** Slipping regular m as you come to them, work in patt to 3 sts before first removable m, M1, remove m and place it on the right needle after the M1 just made, work in patt to the second removable m, remove m, work 3 sts in patt, replace removable m, M1, work in patt to end—2 sts inc'd; each removable m has moved 3 sts outward.

ROW 8: Work even in patt.

Cont in patt, rep the shaping of Rows 5–8 five more times, then work Rows 5 and 6 once more—129 (139, 149, 161, 171) sts; front measures about 4½" (11.5 cm) from sts CO at each side for armholes.

## Shape Shoulders

**note:** *Cowl shaping will still be in progress when shoulder shaping is introduced; read the next sections all the way through before proceeding.*

For cowl shaping, *work Row 7, work 3 rows even, work Row 5, work 3 rows even; rep from * 2 more times, then work Rows 7 and 8 zero (one, one, one, one) more time—12 (14, 14, 14, 14) more sts added to front.

*At the same time,* when front measures 5½ (5½, 6, 6¾, 7¼)" (14 [14, 15, 17, 18.5] cm) from sts CO at each side for armholes, work shoulder shaping as foll, starting with a RS row: BO 4 (5, 5, 6, 7) sts at beg of next 8 rows, then 4 (5, 5, 7, 7) sts at beg of foll 2 rows, then 5 (5, 7, 7, 7) sts at beg of next 2 rows, then 4 (4, 7, 7, 8) sts at beg of next 2 rows—58 (68, 78, 90, 100) sts total removed from front by shoulder shaping; 29 (34, 39, 45, 50) sts from each side.

When all cowl and shoulder shaping has been completed—83 (85, 85, 85, 85) center front sts rem. BO all sts.

# sleeves

With smaller cir needle, CO 43 (43, 45, 47, 49) sts. Work in St st for 6 rows, ending with a RS row. Knit 1 WS row for fold line. Work in St st for 6 rows, ending with a WS row—piece measures about ¾" (2 cm) from fold line. Change to larger cir needle. Work textured stripe patt in rows for 2 rows.

INC ROW: (RS) K1, M1, work in patt to last st, M1, k1—2 sts inc'd.

Cont in patt, rep the inc row every 10 (10, 10, 8, 6) rows 1 (1, 10, 14, 6) more time(s), then every 12 (12, 12, 0, 8) rows 8 (8, 1, 0, 10) time(s), working new sts into patt—63 (63, 69, 77, 83) sts. Work even until piece measures 17½ (17½, 18, 18¼, 18½)" (44.5 [44.5, 45.5, 46.5, 47] cm) from fold line. BO all sts.

# finishing

With yarn threaded on a tapestry needle, sew shoulder seams. Sew short side seams between dividing round and armhole openings. Sew sleeve seams. Sew sleeves into armholes. Fold lower body and cuff hems to WS along fold lines and sew invisibly in place. Using sewing needle and thread, sew three buttons to center of faux placket, the highest about ¾" (2 cm) down from neck edge, the lowest 1" (2.5 cm) up from start of placket, and the middle button centered in between.

Weave in all loose ends. Block lightly to measurements.

# meier CARDIGAN

## FINISHED SIZE

31¾ (34¼, 37, 39¾, 42¼, 45¾, 49½)" (80.5 [87, 94, 101, 107.5, 116, 125.5] cm) bust circumference, including 1" (2.5 cm) front bands. Cardigan shown measures 31¾" (80.5 cm).

## YARN

Worsted Weight (#4 Medium).

**SHOWN HERE:** Berroco *Ultra Alpaca* (50% alpaca, 50% wool; 215 yd [197 m]/ 100 g): #6285 oceanic mix, 4 (4, 5, 5, 5, 6, 6) skeins.

## NEEDLES

**BODY AND SLEEVES**—size U.S. 8 (5 mm): 24" (61 cm) circular (cir) needle.

**RIBBING**—size U.S. 7 (4.5 mm): 24" (61 cm) cir needle.

*Adjust needle sizes, if necessary, to obtain the correct gauge.*

## NOTIONS

Markers (m); stitch holders; tapestry needle; seven ¾" (2 cm) buttons, sewing needle and matching thread.

## GAUGE

18 sts and 25 rows = 4" (10 cm) in St st on larger needle.

25 sts of Side Panel chart measure 6" (15 cm) wide on larger needle.

16 sts and 25 rows = 4" (10 cm) in patt from Sleeve chart on larger needle.

Sometimes I don't feel the need to use an allover pattern to design an interesting garment; instead, I use a portion of a pattern on side panels of the sweater and then repeat the allover pattern on the sleeve. Side panels are knit in one piece with the fronts and back to lessen the headache of sewing perfectly matched side seams, and the waist shaping is worked in the stockinette sections outside the lace panels so you don't need to worry about shaping in pattern. Just relax and enjoy the easy flow of contrasts . . . like a sleek Richard Meier building cropping up among the brownstones.

## stitch guide

### K2, P2 RIB
*(multiple of 4 sts + 2)*

ROW 1: (RS) K2, *p2, k2; rep from *.

ROW 2: (WS) P2, *k2, p2; rep from *.

Rep Rows 1 and 2 for patt.

## note

⊖ When working the dividing row and sleeve shaping, if there are not enough stitches to work both a yarnover and its companion decrease, work the remaining stitch in stockinette to avoid throwing off the stitch count.

# body

With smaller cir needle, CO 138 (150, 162, 174, 186, 202, 218) sts. Work in k2, p2 rib (see Stitch Guide) until piece measures 2" (5 cm), ending with a RS row. Change to larger cir needle.

SETUP ROW: (WS) P20 (24, 28, 31, 33, 38, 42), pm, p25, pm, p48 (52, 56, 62, 70, 76, 84), pm, p25, pm, p20 (24, 28, 31, 33, 38, 42).

NEXT ROW: (RS) *Work in St st to m, slip marker (sl m), work Row 1 of Side Panel chart over 25 sts, sl m; rep from * once more, work in St st to end.

Working 25-st marked side sections in chart patt and rem sts in St st, work 3 rows even, beg and ending with a WS row—piece measures about 2¾" (7 cm) from CO.

## Shape Waist

**note:** *When working the following directions, after completing Row 10 of the chart repeat Rows 11–20 for the pattern.*

DEC ROW: (RS) *Work in St st to 2 sts before m, k2tog, sl m, work 25 chart sts, sl m, ssk; rep from * once more, work in St st to end—4 sts dec'd.

Cont in patt, rep the dec row every 4 rows 6 (6, 6, 4, 4, 4, 4) more times, then every 0 (0, 0, 6, 6, 6, 6) rows 0 (0, 0, 2, 2, 2, 2) times—110 (122, 134, 146, 158, 174, 190) sts; piece measures about 6¾ (6¾, 6¾, 7¼, 7¼, 7¼, 7¼)" [17 [17, 17, 18.5, 18.5, 18.5, 18.5] cm) from CO. Work even as established for 1" (2.5 cm), ending with a WS row.

**INC ROW:** (RS) *Work in St st to m, M1 (see Techniques), sl m, work 25 sts chart sts, sl m, M1; rep from * once more, work in St st to end—4 sts inc'd.

Cont in patt, rep the inc row every 4 rows 5 more times—134 (146, 158, 170, 182, 198, 214) sts. Work even until piece measures 14¾ (14¾, 15, 15¼, 15¼, 15¼, 15¼)" (37.5 [37.5, 38, 38.5, 38.5, 38.5, 38.5] cm) from CO, ending with a WS row.

## Divide for Fronts and Back

**DIVIDING ROW:** (RS) Work 27 (31, 35, 38, 38, 43, 45) sts in patt (see Note), place sts just worked on holder for right front, BO 9 (9, 9, 9, 13, 13, 17) sts for right armhole, work in patt until there are 62 (66, 70, 76, 80, 86, 90) sts on right needle after BO gap, place sts just worked on holder for back, BO 9 (9, 9, 9, 13, 13, 17) sts for left armhole, work in patt to end—27 (31, 35, 38, 38, 43, 45) left front sts rem on needle.

# left front

Change to working all sts in St st. Work 1 WS row even. Beg on the next row, dec 1 st at armhole

edge (beg of RS rows, end of WS row) every row 3 (3, 3, 3, 5, 5) times, then every RS row 1 (1, 2, 2, 2, 1, 2) time(s)—23 (27, 30, 33, 33, 37, 38) sts rem. Work even until armhole measures 3¼ (3½, 3½, 3¾, 3¾, 4, 4)" (8.5 [9, 9, 9.5, 9.5, 10, 10] cm) from dividing row, ending with a RS row.

## Shape Front Neck

BO 5 (6, 7, 8, 7, 8, 9) sts at beg of next WS row, work to end—18 (21, 23, 25, 26, 29, 29) sts rem. Dec 1 st at neck edge (end of RS rows, beg of WS rows) every row 5 (7, 7, 7, 7, 7, 7) times, then every RS row 3 (3, 4, 4, 3, 4, 4) times—10 (11, 12, 14, 16, 18, 18) sts. Work even until armhole measures 7½ (7¾, 8, 8¼, 8½, 8¾, 9)" (19 [19.5, 20.5, 21, 21.5, 22, 23] cm), ending with a WS row.

## Shape Shoulder

BO 3 (4, 4, 5, 6, 6, 6) sts at the beg of the next 2 RS rows, then BO rem 4 (3, 4, 4, 4, 6, 6) sts at beg of foll RS row—no sts rem.

# right front

Return 27 (31, 35, 38, 38, 43, 45) held right front sts to larger cir needle and rejoin yarn with WS

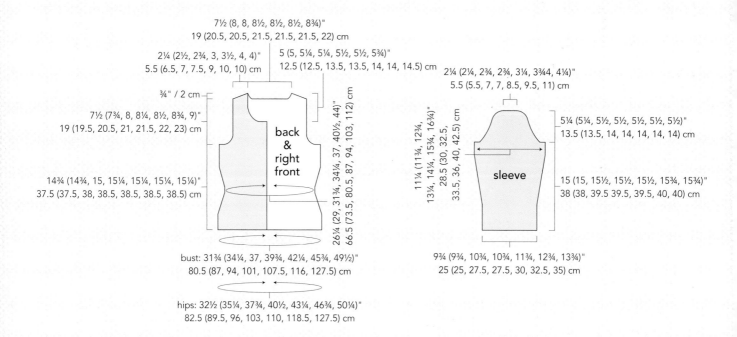

7½ (8, 8, 8½, 8½, 8½, 8¾)"
19 (20.5, 20.5, 21.5, 21.5, 21.5, 22) cm

2¼ (2½, 2¾, 3, 3½, 4, 4)"
5.5 (6.5, 7, 7.5, 9, 10, 10) cm

5 (5, 5¼, 5¼, 5½, 5½, 5¾)"
12.5 (12.5, 13.5, 13.5, 14, 14, 14.5) cm

¾" / 2 cm

7½ (7¾, 8, 8¼, 8½, 8¾, 9)"
19 (19.5, 20.5, 21, 21.5, 22, 23) cm

14¾ (14¾, 15, 15¼, 15¼, 15¼, 15¼)"
37.5 (37.5, 38, 38.5, 38.5, 38.5, 38.5) cm

back & right front

26¼ (29, 31¾, 34¼, 37, 40½, 44)"
66.5 (73.5, 80.5, 87, 94, 103, 112) cm

bust: 31¾ (34¼, 37, 39¾, 42¼, 45¾, 49½)"
80.5 (87, 94, 101, 107.5, 116, 127.5) cm

hips: 32½ (35¼, 37¾, 40½, 43¼, 46¾, 50¼)"
82.5 (89.5, 96, 103, 110, 118.5, 127.5) cm

2¼ (2¼, 2¾, 2¾, 3¼, 3¾, 4¼)"
5.5 (5.5, 7, 7, 8.5, 9.5, 11) cm

5¼ (5¼, 5½, 5½, 5½, 5½, 5½)"
13.5 (13.5, 14, 14, 14, 14, 14) cm

11¼ (11¾, 12¾, 13¾, 14¼, 15¾, 16¾)"
28.5 (30, 32.5, 33.5, 36, 40, 42.5) cm

sleeve

15 (15, 15½, 15½, 15½, 15¾, 15¾)"
38 (38, 39.5 39.5, 39.5, 40, 40) cm

9¾ (9¾, 10¾, 10¾, 11¾, 12¾, 13¾)"
25 (25, 27.5, 27.5, 30, 32.5, 35) cm

facing at armhole edge. Change to working all sts in St st. Work 1 WS row even. Beg on the next row, dec 1 st at armhole edge (end of RS rows, beg of WS row) every row 3 (3, 3, 3, 5, 5) times, then every RS row 1 (1, 2, 2, 2, 1, 2) time(s)—23 (27, 30, 33, 33, 37, 38) sts rem. Work even until armhole measures 3¼ (3½, 3½, 3¾, 3¾, 4, 4)" (8.5 [9, 9, 9.5, 9.5, 10, 10] cm) from dividing row, ending with a WS row.

## Shape Front Neck

BO 5 (6, 7, 8, 7, 8, 9) sts at beg of next RS row, work to end—18 (21, 23, 25, 26, 29, 29) sts. Dec 1 st at neck edge (beg of RS rows, end of WS rows) every row 5 (7, 7, 7, 7, 7, 7) times, then every RS row 3 (3, 4, 4, 3, 4, 4) times—10 (11, 12, 14, 16, 18, 18) sts. Work even until armhole measures 7½ (7¾, 8, 8¼, 8½, 8¾, 9)" (19 [19.5, 20.5, 21, 21.5, 22, 23] cm), ending with a RS row.

## Shape Shoulder

BO 3 (4, 4, 5, 6, 6, 6) sts at the beg of the next 2 WS rows, then BO rem 4 (3, 4, 4, 4, 6, 6) sts at beg of foll WS row—no sts rem.

# back

Return 62 (66, 70, 76, 80, 86, 90) held back sts to larger cir needle and rejoin yarn with WS facing. Change to working all sts in St st. Work 1 WS row even. Dec 1 st at each armhole edge every

row 3 (3, 3, 3, 3, 5, 5) times, then every RS row 1 (1, 2, 2, 2, 1, 2) time(s)—54 (58, 60, 66, 70, 74, 76) sts. Work even until armhole measures 7½ (7¾, 8, 8¼, 8½, 8¾, 9)" (19 [19.5, 20.5, 21, 21.5, 22, 23] cm), ending with a WS row.

## Shape Shoulders and Back Neck

NEXT ROW: (RS) BO 3 (4, 4, 5, 6, 6, 6) sts, work until there are 9 (9, 10, 11, 12, 14, 14) sts on right needle after BO, place rem 42 (45, 46, 50, 52, 54, 56) sts on holder—9 (9, 10, 11, 12, 14, 14) right back shoulder sts rem on needle.

### Right back shoulder

NEXT ROW: (WS) P2tog at neck edge, work to end—8 (8, 9, 10, 11, 13, 13) sts.

NEXT ROW: (RS) BO 3 (4, 4, 5, 6, 6, 6) sts, work to last 2 sts, k2tog—4 (3, 4, 4, 4, 6, 6) sts.

NEXT ROW: Work even.

BO all sts with RS facing.

### Left back shoulder

Return 42 (45, 46, 50, 52, 54, 56) held sts to larger cir needle and rejoin yarn with RS facing.

NEXT ROW: (RS) BO 30 (32, 32, 34, 34, 34, 36) sts for back neck, work to end—12 (13, 14, 16, 18, 20, 20) sts.

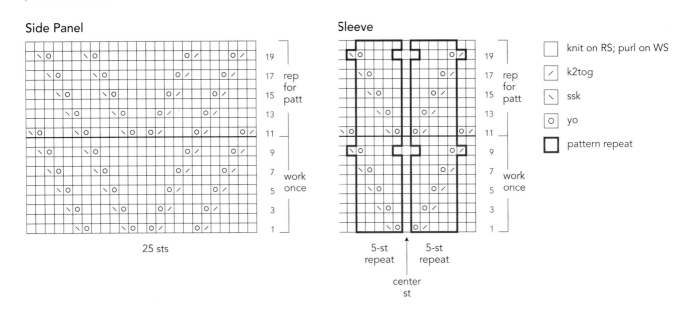

Side Panel

25 sts

Sleeve

5-st repeat    5-st repeat

center st

knit on RS; purl on WS

k2tog

ssk

yo

pattern repeat

NEXT ROW: (WS) BO 3 (4, 4, 5, 6, 6, 6) sts, work to last 2 sts, ssp (see Techniques) at neck edge—8 (8, 9, 10, 11, 13, 13) sts.

NEXT ROW: Ssk (see Techniques), work to end—7 (7, 8, 9, 10, 12, 12) sts.

NEXT ROW: BO 3 (4, 4, 5, 6, 6, 6) sts, work to end—4 (3, 4, 4, 4, 6, 6) sts.

BO all sts with RS facing.

## sleeves

With smaller cir needle, CO 38 (38, 42, 42, 46, 50, 54) sts. Work k2, p2 rib until piece measures 2½" (6.5 cm), ending with a WS row, and *at the same time* inc 1 st in last row—39 (39, 43, 43, 47, 51, 55) sts. Change to larger cir needle.

Establish patt from Row 1 of Sleeve chart as foll: (RS) K2 (2, 4, 4, 1, 3, 0), work 2 sts before first patt rep once, work first 5-st patt rep 3 (3, 3, 3, 4, 4, 5) times, work center st once, work second 5-st patt rep 3 (3, 3, 3, 4, 4, 5) times, work 2 sts after second rep once, k2 (2, 4, 4, 1, 3, 0).

**note:** *When working the following directions, after completing Row 10 of the chart repeat Rows 11–20 for the pattern.*

Working any sts on each side of chart section in St st, work even as established until piece measures 4½" (11.5 cm) from CO, ending with a WS row.

INC ROW: (RS) K1, M1, work in patt to last st, M1, k1—2 sts inc'd.

Cont in patt, rep the inc row every 26 (18, 18, 14, 14, 12, 12) rows 2 (3, 3, 4, 4, 5, 5) times, working new sts into chart patt (see Notes)—45 (47, 51, 53, 57, 63, 67) sts. Work even in patt until piece measures 15 (15, 15½, 15½, 15½, 15¾, 15¾)" (38 [38, 39.5, 39.5, 39.5, 40, 40] cm), ending with a WS row.

### Shape Sleeve Cap

BO 5 (5, 5, 5, 7, 7, 9) sts at beg of next 2 rows—35 (37, 41, 43, 43, 49, 49) sts. Dec 1 st each end of needle every RS row 2 (2, 3, 3, 3, 2, 3) times, every 4 rows 4 (4, 4, 4, 4, 4, 3) times, every RS row 4 (3, 3, 2, 3, 2, 5) times, then every row 1 (3, 3, 5, 3, 7, 3) time(s)—13 (13, 15, 15, 17, 19, 21) sts rem. BO 2 sts at beg of next 2 rows—9 (9, 11, 11, 13, 15, 17) sts. BO all sts.

# finishing

Block pieces to measurements. With yarn threaded on a tapestry needle, sew shoulder seams. Sew sleeve seams. Sew sleeve caps into armholes.

## Buttonband

With smaller cir needle and RS facing, pick up and knit 78 (82, 82, 86, 86, 86, 86) sts along left front edge. Work in k2, p2 rib for 7 rows, beg and ending with a WS row. With RS facing, BO all sts in patt.

## Buttonhole Band

With smaller cir needle and RS facing, pick up and knit 78 (82, 82, 86, 86, 86, 86) sts along right front edge. Work in k2, p2 rib for 3 rows, beg and ending with a WS row.

BUTTONHOLE ROW: (RS) Work 5 (4, 4, 3, 3, 3, 3) sts in rib patt, *work 3-st one-row buttonhole (see Techniques), work 9 (10, 10, 11, 11, 11, 11) sts in rib patt; rep from * 4 more times, work 3-st one-row buttonhole, work 10 sts in rib patt for all sizes—6 buttonholes completed.

**note:** *The seventh buttonhole will be worked in the neckband.*

Work in k2, p2 rib for 3 rows, ending with a WS row. BO all sts in patt.

## Neckband

With smaller cir needle and RS facing, pick up and knit 110 (110, 110, 114, 118, 118, 122) sts around neck opening. Work in k2, p2 rib for 3 rows, beg and ending with a WS row.

BUTTONHOLE ROW: (RS) Work 3 sts in rib patt, work 3-st one-row buttonhole, work in rib patt to end.

Work in k2, p2 rib for 3 rows, ending with a WS row. BO all sts in patt.

Weave in all loose ends. Block again, if desired. Using sewing needle and thread, sew buttons to buttonband, opposite buttonholes.

# open air PULLOVER

## FINISHED SIZE

32 (34, 36, 38½, 40½, 44, 48)" (81.5 [86.5, 91.5, 98, 103, 112, 122] cm) bust circumference. Pullover shown measures 34" (86.5 cm).

## YARN

Fingering Weight (#1 Super Fine).

**SHOWN HERE:** Hand Maiden *Mini Maiden* (50% silk, 50% wool; 547 yd [500 m]/ 100 g): pumpkin, 3 (3, 3, 4, 4, 4, 5) skeins.

## NEEDLES

**BODY AND SLEEVES**—size U.S. 4 (3.5 mm): 16" and 24" (40.5 and 61 cm) circular (cir) needles.

**RIBBING**—size U.S. 3 (3.25 mm): 24" (61 cm) cir needle.

*Adjust needle sizes, if necessary, to obtain the correct gauge.*

## NOTIONS

Markers (m); stitch holders; sewing needle and matching thread; tapestry needle; four ⅝" (1.5 cm) buttons.

## GAUGE

25 sts and 32 rows = 4" (10 cm) in St st on larger needle.

29 sts and 36 rows/rnds = 4" (10 cm) in k2, p2 rib on smaller needle, with rib relaxed so that each p2 column appears about 1 st wide.

Surplice silhouettes look great on so many different body types, but sadly they tend to be hard to find in the stores: they lack what those in the industry call "hanger appeal." If it looks bad on the hanger, shoppers tend to pass it by so the stores pass on the orders. A lightweight, beautifully drapey yarn, high-rib start, faux button placket, and gathering at the shoulders all come together in concert for a perfect addition to your wardrobe that can be worn day or night—and will drape gorgeously as you stroll around town.

# stitch guide

## NECK EDGE
*(worked over 5 sts)*

AT BEG OF BOTH RS AND WS ROWS: [Sl 1 pwise wyf, k1] 2 times, sl 1 pwise wyf.

AT END OF BOTH RS AND WS ROWS: [K1, sl 1 pwise wyf] 2 times, kl.

## K2, P2 RIB IN ROWS
*(multiple of 4 sts + 2)*

ROW 1: (RS) K2, *p2, k2; rep from * to end.

ROW 2: (WS) P2, *k2, p2; rep from * to end.

Rep Rows 1 and 2 for patt.

# notes

⊖ The deep lower body ribbing is worked in the round in k2, p2 rib with a section of k1, p1 rib for a faux button placket. Above the ribbing, the center front stitches are doubled, and half the stitches in the doubled section are transferred to a separate needle for the underlap of the surplice front. The body changes to working back and forth in rows to the armholes, then the fronts and back are divided for working separately to the shoulders. The sleeves are worked back and forth in rows.

⊖ I wanted to work the lower body in the round to minimize seams, so the surplice is worked in an interesting way, working both overlapping layers at the same time. The first row or two is a little challenging, but well worth the finished outcome.

⊖ The back shoulders are sloped, but the front shoulders are worked straight across with ribbed details that gather the fronts softly below the shoulder seams.

⊖ The faux button placket is not only easier to work but gives a smooth fit. When a placket is worked in a section of a sweater that stretches, such as the ribbed waist here or the fullest part of a cardigan bust, a functional placket may pull and gape between the buttons. If the placket doesn't have to unbutton, why risk letting it ruin the straight, clean lines of your sweater?

# body

## Lower Body Rib

With smaller cir needle, CO 197 (209, 225, 245, 257, 285, 317) sts. Place marker (pm) and join for working in rnds; the rnd begins at left side at start of the front sts.

**NEXT RND:** [K2, p2] 6 (6, 7, 7, 8, 9, 9) times, pm, work next 7 sts for faux placket as [k1, p1] 3 times, k1, pm, *p2, k2; rep from * to last 2 sts, p2.

Work sts as they appear (knit the knits and purl the purls) until piece measures 5½" (14 cm).

## Lower Body

Change to longer cir needle in larger size.

**DEC RND:** Removing m on each side of faux placket as you come to them, k7 (3, 3, 9, 7, 13, 17), [k2tog, k7 (8, 7, 6, 6, 6, 5)] 20 (20, 24, 28, 30, 32, 40) times, k2tog, k8 (4, 4, 10, 8, 14, 18)—176 (188, 200, 216, 226, 252, 276) sts.

**NEXT RND:** K20 (22, 24, 27, 28, 33, 37), work k1f&b (see Techniques) 48 (50, 52, 54, 56, 60, 64) times, k20 (22, 24, 27, 28, 33, 37), pm for right side, k88 (94, 100, 108, 114, 126, 138) back sts—224 (238, 252, 270, 282, 312, 340) sts.

Arrange sts for working back and forth in rows as foll: K20 (22, 24, 27, 28, 33, 37) to beg of k1f&b sts, and temporarily drop working yarn. With shorter cir needle held in front of work, [sl next st to shorter cir needle, sl foll st to end of longer cir needle] 48 (50, 52, 54, 56, 60, 64) times. With the shorter cir needle dangling in front of work, return 48 (50, 52, 54, 56, 60, 64) slipped sts to left tip of longer cir needle, and knit across them—68 (72, 76, 81, 84, 93, 101) sts each front; 88 (94, 100, 108, 114, 126, 138) back sts; 48 (50, 52, 54, 56, 60, 64) sts at right front edge are on shorter cir needle.

Turn work so WS is facing.

**NEXT ROW:** (WS) P68 (72, 76, 81, 84, 93, 101) left front sts to side m, sl m, p88 (94, 100, 108, 114, 126, 138) back sts, sl m, purl to last 5 right front sts, work neck edge (see Stitch Guide) over 5 sts.

**NEXT ROW:** (RS) Work neck edge over first 5 right front sts, knit to last 5 sts, work neck edge over last 5 left front sts.

NEXT ROW: (WS) Work neck edge over first 5 left front sts, purl to last 5 sts, work neck edge over last 5 right front sts—piece measures 6" (15 cm) from CO.

## Shape Bust and Neck

**Note:** *Work the following instructions using both circular needles until you can comfortably transfer all the stitches to the longer circular needle. Continue the neck edge as established all the way to the end of the fronts.*

**Note:** *The neck decreases are worked at the same time as the bust increases; read the next sections all the way through before proceeding.*

NEXT ROW: (RS) Work 5 sts neck edge, ssk, *work to 1 st before side m, M1 (see Techniques), k1, slip marker (sl m), k1, M1; rep from * once more, work to last 7 sts, k2tog, work 5 sts neck edge—226 (240, 254, 272, 284, 314, 342) sts total; still 68 (72, 76, 81, 84, 93, 101) sts each front (the 1 st bust inc offsets the 1 st neck dec); 90 (96, 102, 110, 116, 128, 140) back sts.

Shape bust by inc 1 st on each side of both side m as in the previous row every 10 (10, 12, 12, 14, 14, 14) rows 1 (1, 3, 1, 4, 4, 2) more time(s), then every 12 (12, 14, 14, 16, 16, 16) rows 4 (4, 2, 4, 1, 1, 3) time(s), working new sts in St st—20 sts total added for bust: 10 back sts, and 5 sts each front.

*At the same time,* dec 1 st on both right and left fronts inside neck edging as in the previous row every 4 rows 16 (16, 17, 15, 9, 10, 10) times, then every 6 rows 0 (0, 0, 2, 6, 6, 6) times—16 (16, 17, 17, 15, 16, 16) more sts removed from each neck edge.

When this shaping has been completed—214 (228, 240, 258, 274, 302, 330) sts total; 57 (61, 64, 69, 74, 82, 90) sts each front; 100 (106, 112, 120, 126, 138, 150) back sts; piece measures about 14 (14, 14½, 15, 15, 15½, 15½)" (35.5 [35.5, 37, 38, 38, 39.5, 39.5] cm) from CO.

Work even if necessary for your size until piece measures 14 (14, 14½, 15, 15½, 15½, 16)" (35.5 [35.5, 37, 38, 39.5, 39.5, 40.5] cm) from CO, ending with a WS row.

## Divide for Fronts and Back

NEXT ROW: (RS) Removing side m as you come to them, *work to 6 (7, 7, 8, 8, 10, 12) sts before

side m, BO 12 (14, 14, 16, 16, 20, 24) underarm sts; rep from * once more, work to end—51 (54, 57, 61, 66, 72, 78) sts each front; 88 (92, 98, 104, 110, 118, 126) back sts.

Place sts for back and right front on separate holders.

# left front

**note:** *Neck shaping continues while armhole shaping is introduced; read the next sections all the way through before proceeding.*

Cont on 51 (54, 57, 61, 66, 72, 78) left front sts. Work 1 WS row even.

Beg on the next RS row, for armhole shaping dec 1 st at armhole edge (beg of RS rows, end of WS rows) every row 5 (5, 5, 7, 7, 9, 12) times—5 (5, 5, 7, 7, 9, 12) sts removed at armhole edge.

*At the same time,* cont neck shaping by dec 1 st at each neck edge every 4 rows 12 (11, 1, 0, 0, 0, 0) time(s), then every 6 rows 0 (0, 7, 8, 9, 9, 10) times—12 (11, 8, 8, 9, 9, 10) more sts removed from each neck edge.

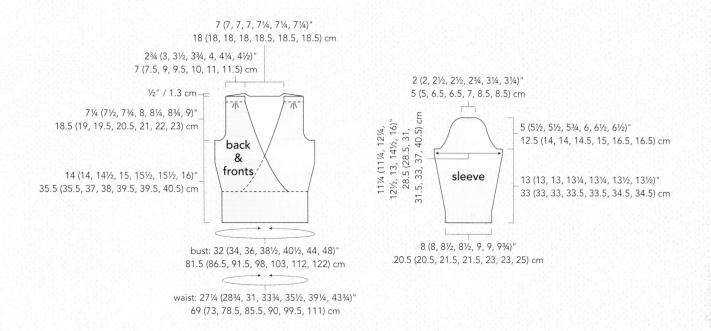

7 (7, 7, 7, 7¼, 7¼, 7¼)"
18 (18, 18, 18, 18.5, 18.5, 18.5) cm

2¾ (3, 3½, 3¾, 4, 4¼, 4½)"
7 (7.5, 9, 9.5, 10, 11, 11.5) cm

½" / 1.3 cm

7¼ (7½, 7¾, 8, 8¼, 8¾, 9)"
18.5 (19, 19.5, 20.5, 21, 22, 23) cm

back & fronts

14 (14, 14½, 15, 15½, 15½, 16)"
35.5 (35.5, 37, 38, 39.5, 39.5, 40.5) cm

bust: 32 (34, 36, 38½, 40½, 44, 48)"
81.5 (86.5, 91.5, 98, 103, 112, 122) cm

waist: 27¼ (28¾, 31, 33¾, 35½, 39¼, 43¾)"
69 (73, 78.5, 85.5, 90, 99.5, 111) cm

2 (2, 2½, 2½, 2¾, 3¼, 3¼)"
5 (5, 6.5, 6.5, 7, 8.5, 8.5) cm

11¼ (11¼, 12¼, 12½, 13, 14½, 16)"
28.5 (28.5, 31, 31.5, 33, 37, 40.5) cm

sleeve

5 (5½, 5½, 5¾, 6, 6½, 6½)"
12.5 (14, 14, 14.5, 15, 16.5, 16.5) cm

13 (13, 13, 13¼, 13¼, 13½, 13½)"
33 (33, 33, 33.5, 33.5, 34.5, 34.5) cm

8 (8, 8½, 8½, 9, 9, 9¾)"
20.5 (20.5, 21.5, 21.5, 23, 23, 25) cm

When this shaping has been completed—34 (38, 44, 46, 50, 54, 56) sts rem. Work even until armhole measures 6¼ (6½, 6¾, 7, 7¼, 7¾, 8)" (16 [16.5, 17, 18, 18.5, 19.5, 20.5] cm), ending with a WS row.

NEXT ROW: (RS) K2 (3, 3, 5, 6, 7, 6), [k1, k2tog] 9 (10, 12, 12, 13, 14, 15) times, work 5 neck edge sts—25 (28, 32, 34, 37, 40, 41) sts.

NEXT ROW: (WS) Purl.

NEXT ROW: (RS) K4 (5, 7, 7, 8, 9, 10), [k2tog] 8 (9, 10, 11, 12, 13, 13) times, work 5 neck edge sts—17 (19, 22, 23, 25, 27, 28) sts.

NEXT ROW: (WS) P1, *k1, p1; rep from * to end.

Work sts in established k1, p1 rib patt for ½" (1.3 cm), ending with a WS row—armhole measures 7¼ (7½, 7¾, 8, 8¼, 8¾, 9)" (18.5 [19, 19.5, 20.5, 21, 22, 23] cm). BO all sts in patt.

# right front

note: As for left front, neck shaping is worked at the same time as armhole shaping; read the next sections all the way through before proceeding.

Return 51 (54, 57, 61, 66, 72, 78) held right front sts to larger cir needle and rejoin yarn with WS facing. Work 1 WS row even.

Beg on the next RS row, for armhole shaping dec 1 st at armhole edge (end of RS rows, beg of WS rows) every row 5 (5, 5, 7, 7, 9, 12) times—5 (5, 5, 7, 7, 9, 12) sts removed at armhole edge.

At the same time, cont neck shaping by dec 1 st at each neck edge every 4 rows 12 (11, 1, 0, 0, 0, 0) time(s), then every 6 rows 0 (0, 7, 8, 9, 9, 10) times—12 (11, 8, 8, 9, 9, 10) more sts removed from each neck edge.

When this shaping has been completed—34 (38, 44, 46, 50, 54, 56) sts rem. Work even until armhole measures 6¼ (6½, 6¾, 7, 7¼, 7¾, 8)" (16 [16.5, 17, 18, 18.5, 19.5, 20.5] cm), ending with a WS row.

NEXT ROW: (RS) Work 5 neck edge sts, [k1, k2tog] 9 (10, 12, 12, 13, 14, 15) times, k2 (3, 3, 5, 6, 7, 6)—25 (28, 32, 32, 34, 37, 40, 41) sts.

NEXT ROW: (WS) Purl.

NEXT ROW: (RS) Work 5 neck edge sts, [k2tog] 8 (9, 10, 11, 12, 13, 13) times, k4 (5, 7, 7, 8, 9, 10)—17 (19, 22, 23, 25, 27, 28) sts.

NEXT ROW: (WS) P1, *k1, p1; rep from * to end.

Work sts in established k1, p1 rib patt for ½" (1.3 cm), ending with a WS row—armhole measures 7¼ (7½, 7¾, 8, 8¼, 8¾, 9)" (18.5 [19, 19.5, 20.5, 21, 22, 23] cm). BO all sts in patt.

# back

Return 88 (92, 98, 104, 110, 118, 126) held back sts to larger cir needle and rejoin yarn with WS facing. Work 1 WS row even. Dec 1 st at each armhole edge every row 5 (5, 5, 7, 7, 9, 12) times—78 (82, 88, 90, 96, 100, 102) sts rem. Work even until armholes measure 7¼ (7½, 7¾, 8, 8¼, 8¾, 9)" (18.5 [19, 19.5, 20.5, 21, 22, 23] cm), ending with a WS row.

## Shape Shoulders and Back Neck

NEXT ROW: (RS) BO 6 (6, 7, 8, 8, 9, 10) sts, knit until there are 14 (16, 18, 18, 20, 21, 21) sts on right needle after BO, place remaining 58 (60, 63, 64, 68, 70, 71) sts on holder—14 (16, 18, 18, 20, 21, 21) right shoulder sts rem on needle.

### Right back shoulder

NEXT ROW: (WS) P2tog at neck edge, purl to end—13 (15, 17, 17, 19, 20, 20) sts.

NEXT ROW: BO 6 (6, 7, 8, 9, 9, 10) sts, knit to last 2 sts, k2tog—6 (8, 9, 8, 9, 10, 9) sts.

NEXT ROW: P2tog, purl to end—5 (7, 8, 7, 8, 9, 8) sts.

BO rem sts.

### Left back shoulder

Return 58 (60, 63, 64, 68, 70, 71) held sts to larger cir needle and rejoin yarn with RS facing.

NEXT ROW: (RS) BO 38 (38, 38, 38, 40, 40, 40) sts, knit to end—20 (22, 25, 26, 28, 30, 31) sts.

NEXT ROW: (WS) BO 6 (6, 7, 8, 8, 9, 10) sts, purl to last 2 sts, ssp (see Techniques)—13 (15, 17, 17, 19, 20, 20) sts.

NEXT ROW: Ssk (see Techniques), knit to end—12 (14, 16, 16, 18, 19, 19) sts.

NEXT ROW: BO 6 (6, 7, 8, 9, 9, 10) sts, purl to last 2 sts, ssp—5 (7, 8, 7, 8, 9, 8) sts.

BO rem sts.

# sleeves

With smaller cir needle, CO 58 (58, 62, 62, 66, 66, 70) sts. Work k2, p2 rib in rows (see Stitch Guide) until piece measures 2" (5 cm), ending with a WS row. Change to longer cir needle in larger size. Work in St st and inc 1 st at each side every 14 (14, 10, 10, 10, 6, 6) rows 6 (6, 2, 6, 6, 6, 15) times, then every 0 (0, 12, 12, 12, 8, 0) rows 0 (0, 5, 2, 2, 6, 0) times, working new sts in St st—70 (70, 76, 78, 82, 90, 100) sts. Work even until sleeve measures 13 (13, 13, 13¼, 13¼, 13½, 13½)" (33 [33, 33, 33.5, 33.5, 34.5, 34.5] cm), ending with a WS row.

## Shape Sleeve Cap

BO 6 (7, 7, 8, 8, 10, 12) sts at beg of next 2 rows—58 (56, 62, 62, 66, 70, 76) sts rem. Dec 1 st each end of needle every RS row 5 (3, 4, 3, 4, 4, 7) times, every 4 rows 3 (5, 5, 5, 5, 7, 3) times, every RS row 3 (4, 2, 5, 5, 2, 8) times, then every row 9 (7, 9, 7, 7, 9, 7) times—18 (18, 22, 22, 24, 26, 26) sts. BO 3 sts at the beginning of the next 2 rows—12 (12, 16, 16, 18, 20, 20) sts. BO rem sts.

# finishing

Block pieces to measurements. With yarn threaded on a tapestry needle, sew shoulder seams. Sew sleeve seams. Sew sleeves into armholes. Weave in all loose ends. Using sewing needle and thread, sew four buttons along center line of faux placket as shown, with the lowest button about ½" (1.3 cm) up from the CO edge, the highest ½" (1.3 cm) down from the top of the lower body rib, and the rem buttons evenly spaced in between.

# skyline TUNIC

## FINISHED SIZE
34 (36½, 38½, 40½, 44, 48)" (86.5 [92.5, 98, 103, 112, 122] cm) bust circumference. Pullover shown measures 34" (86.5 cm).

## YARN
Worsted Weight (#4 Medium).

**SHOWN HERE:** Valley Yarns *Amherst* (100% merino wool; 109 yd [100 m]/50 g): charcoal, 10 (11, 11, 12, 13, 14) balls.

## NEEDLES
**BODY AND SLEEVES**—size U.S. 8 (5 mm): 24" (61 cm) circular (cir) needle.

**RIBBING**—size U.S. 7 (4.5 mm): 16" and 24" (40.5 and 61 cm) cir needles.

*Adjust needle sizes, if necessary, to obtain the correct gauge.*

## NOTIONS
Markers (m); stitch holder; tapestry needle.

## GAUGE
17 sts and 24 rows = 4" (10 cm) in St st on larger needle.

23 sts of Argyle Lace chart measure 5½" (14 cm) wide on larger needle.

Tunics are one of my favorite wardrobe staples. I think of them as "fashionable sweatshirts." They can be worn as a top over skinny jeans or as a dress over tights or leggings. In this piece, I especially love the asymmetrical placement of the almost argylelike lace pattern, which takes a classic design element and gives it a bit of a twist. Like the Manhattan skyline, it's stately, artistic, intriguing, and will easily outlast any trend.

## stitch guide

### K2, P2 RIB
*(multiple of 4 sts + 2)*

ROW 1: (RS) K2, *p2, k2; rep from *.

ROW 2: (WS) P2, *k2, p2; rep from *.

Rep Rows 1 and 2 for patt.

### SLOPED SHOULDER BIND-OFF

I prefer to bind off the shoulder stitches using the sloped shoulder method to eliminate the "stair steps" along the shoulder edge. Work the first BO row as normal, then work 1 row even. On the next BO row, slip the first st knitwise, knit the next st, then pass the slipped st over the knit st to BO 1 st, then work the rest of the BO sts as normal.

## note

⊖ During shaping, if there are not enough stitches in the chart section to work a decrease with its companion yarnover, work the remaining stitch in stockinette instead.

## back

With longer cir needle in smaller size, CO 86 (90, 94, 102, 110, 122) sts. Work k2, p2 rib (see Stitch Guide) until piece measures 4" (10 cm), ending with a WS row. Change to larger cir needle, and cont in St st as foll:

NEXT ROW: (RS) K6 (10, 4, 6, 2, 10), [k2tog, k6 (6, 7, 6, 7, 6)] 10 (10, 10, 12, 12, 14) times—76 (80, 84, 90, 98, 108) sts.

Work even in St st until piece measures 7" (18 cm) from CO, ending with a WS row.

### Shape Waist

DEC ROW: (RS) K1, ssk (see Techniques), work to last 3 sts, k2tog, k1—2 sts dec'd.

Cont in St st, rep the dec row every 6 (6, 6, 4, 6, 4) rows 6 (6, 5, 2, 4, 1) more time(s), then every 0 (0, 8, 6, 8, 6) rows 0 (0, 1, 5, 2, 6) time(s)—62 (66, 70, 74, 84, 92) sts rem; piece measures about 13¼ (13¼, 13½, 13½, 13¾, 13¾)" (33.5 [33.5, 34.5, 34.5, 35, 35] cm) from CO. Work even for 7 rows, beg and ending with a WS row.

INC ROW: (RS) K1, M1 (see Techniques), work to last st, M1, k1—2 sts inc'd.

Cont in St st, rep the inc row every 8 (6, 6, 6, 8, 8) rows 4 (4, 4, 4, 3, 3) more times, then every 0 (8, 8, 8, 10, 10) rows 0 (1, 1, 1, 1, 1) time(s)—72 (78, 82, 86, 94, 102) sts. Work even until piece measures 20½ (20½, 21, 21, 21½, 21½)" (52 [52, 53.5, 53.5, 54.5, 54.5] cm) from CO ending with a WS row.

### Shape Armholes

BO 4 (5, 6, 6, 7, 9) sts at beg of next 2 rows—64 (68, 70, 74, 80, 84) sts. Dec 1 st at each side every row 4 (4, 4, 5, 6, 6) times—56 (60, 62, 64, 68, 72) sts rem. Work even until armholes measure 7¾ (8, 8¼, 8½, 8¾, 9)" (19.5 [20.5, 21, 21.5, 22, 23] cm), ending with a WS row.

### Shape Shoulders and Back Neck

note: *During the following shaping, use the sloped shoulder bind-off method (see Stitch Guide), if desired.*

**NEXT ROW:** (RS) BO 4 (5, 5, 5, 6, 6) sts, knit until there are 11 (11, 12, 12, 13, 15) sts on right needle after BO, place rem 41 (44, 45, 47, 49, 51) sts on holder—11 (11, 12, 12, 13, 15) right shoulder sts rem on needle.

### Right back shoulder

**NEXT ROW:** (WS) P2tog at neck edge, work to end—10 (10, 11, 11, 12, 14) sts.

**NEXT ROW:** (RS) BO 4 (5, 5, 5, 6, 6) sts, work to last 2 sts, k2tog—5 (4, 5, 5, 5, 7) sts.

**NEXT ROW:** Work even.

BO rem sts with RS facing.

### Left back shoulder

Return 41 (44, 45, 47, 49, 51) held sts to needle and rejoin yarn with RS facing.

**NEXT ROW:** (RS) BO 26 (28, 28, 30, 30, 30) back neck sts, work to end—15 (16, 17, 17, 19, 21) sts.

**NEXT ROW:** (WS) BO 4 (5, 5, 5, 6, 6) sts, work to last 2 sts, ssp (see Techniques) at neck edge—10 (10, 11, 11, 12, 14) sts.

**NEXT ROW:** Ssk (see Techniques), work to end—9 (9, 10, 10, 11, 13) sts.

**NEXT ROW:** BO 4 (5, 5, 5, 6, 6) sts, work to end—5 (4, 5, 5, 5, 7) sts.

**NEXT ROW:** Work even.

BO rem sts with RS facing.

# front

With longer cir needle in smaller size, CO 86 (90, 94, 102, 110, 122) sts. Work k2, p2 rib until piece measures 4" (10 cm), ending with a WS row. Change to larger cir needle, and cont in St st as foll:

**NEXT ROW:** (RS) K6 (10, 4, 6, 2, 10), [k2tog, k6 (6, 7, 6, 7, 6)] 10 (10, 10, 12, 12, 14) times—76 (80, 84, 90, 98, 108) sts.

**NEXT ROW:** (WS) Purl.

**NEXT ROW:** K11 (12, 13, 14, 17, 20), place marker (pm), work Row 1 of Argyle Lace chart over 23 sts, pm, k42 (45, 48, 53, 58, 65).

Working sts outside chart section in St st, cont in patt until piece measures 7" (18 cm) from CO, ending with a WS row.

## Argyle Lace

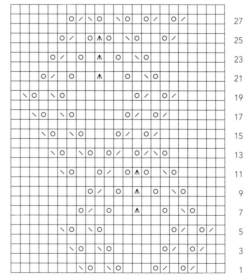

knit on RS; purl on WS

✓ k2tog

\ ssk

⋀ sl 2 as if to k2tog, k1, p2sso

○ yo

23 sts

## Shape Waist

Cont in patt, shape waist as for back—72 (78, 82, 86, 94, 102) sts. Work even until piece measures 20½ (20½, 21, 21, 21½, 21½)" (52 [52, 53.5, 53.5, 54.5, 54.5] cm) from CO ending with a WS row.

## Shape Armholes

Cont in patt (see Note), work as for back—56 (60, 62, 64, 68, 72) sts rem; armholes measure about 1 (1, 1, 1¼, 1½, 1½)" (2.5 [2.5, 2.5, 3.2, 3.8, 3.8] cm). Work even until armholes measure 1½ (1½, 1¾, 1¾, 1¾, 2)" (3.8 [3.8, 4.5, 4.5, 4.5, 5] cm), ending with a WS row.

## Shape Front Neck and Shoulders

NEXT ROW: (RS) Work 24 (26, 27, 28, 30, 32) sts in patt and place sts just worked on holder for left neck, BO 8 center front sts, k24 (26, 27, 28, 30, 32)—24 (26, 27, 28, 30, 32) right neck sts rem on needle.

### Right front neck and shoulder

NEXT ROW: (WS) Work to last 2 sts, ssp at neck edge—1 st dec'd.

NEXT ROW: (RS) Ssk, work to end—1 st dec'd.

Dec 1 st at neck edge (beg of RS rows, end of WS rows) in this manner every row 4 more times, then every RS row 2 times, then every 4 rows 3 (4, 4, 5, 5, 5) times—13 (14, 15, 15, 17, 19) sts rem. Work even until armhole measures 7¾ (8, 8¼, 8½, 8¾, 9)" (19.5 [20.5, 21, 21.5, 22, 23] cm), ending with a RS row. BO 4 (5, 5, 5, 6, 6) sts at beg of next 2 WS rows, then BO 5 (4, 5, 5, 5, 7) sts at beg of foll WS row—no sts rem.

### Left front neck and shoulder

Return 24 (26, 27, 28, 30, 32) held sts to needle and rejoin yarn with WS facing.

NEXT ROW: (WS) P2tog at neck edge, work to end—1 st dec'd.

NEXT ROW: (RS) Work to last 2 sts, k2tog—1 st dec'd.

Dec 1 st at neck edge (end of RS rows, beg of WS rows) in this manner every row 4 more times, then every RS row 2 times, then every 4 rows 3 (4, 4, 5, 5, 5) times—13 (14, 15, 15, 17, 19) sts rem. Work even until armhole measures

7¾ (8, 8¼, 8½, 8¾, 9)" (19.5 [20.5, 21, 21.5, 22, 23] cm), ending with a WS row. BO 4 (5, 5, 5, 6, 6) sts at beg of next 2 RS rows, then BO 5 (4, 5, 5, 5, 7) sts at beg of foll RS row—no sts rem.

## sleeves

With longer cir needle in smaller size, CO 38 (42, 42, 46, 50, 50) sts. Work k2, p2 until piece measures 4" (10 cm), ending with a WS row. Change to larger cir needle, and cont in St st as foll:

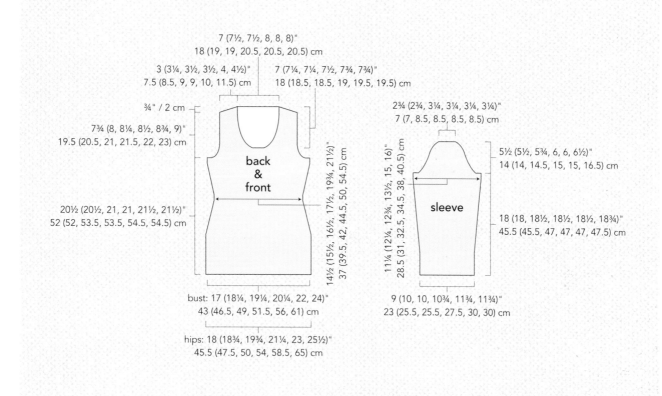

7 (7½, 7½, 8, 8, 8)"
18 (19, 19, 20.5, 20.5, 20.5) cm

3 (3¼, 3½, 3½, 4, 4½)"
7.5 (8.5, 9, 9, 10, 11.5) cm

7 (7¼, 7¼, 7½, 7¾, 7¾)"
18 (18.5, 18.5, 19, 19.5, 19.5) cm

¾" / 2 cm

7¾ (8, 8¼, 8½, 8¾, 9)"
19.5 (20.5, 21, 21.5, 22, 23) cm

back & front

14½ (15½, 16½, 17½, 19¾, 21½)"
37 (39.5, 42, 44.5, 50, 54.5) cm

20½ (20½, 21, 21, 21½, 21½)"
52 (52, 53.5, 53.5, 54.5, 54.5) cm

bust: 17 (18¼, 19¼, 20¼, 22, 24)"
43 (46.5, 49, 51.5, 56, 61) cm

hips: 18 (18¾, 19¾, 21¼, 23, 25½)"
45.5 (47.5, 50, 54, 58.5, 65) cm

2¾ (2¾, 3¼, 3¼, 3¼, 3¼)"
7 (7, 8.5, 8.5, 8.5, 8.5) cm

5½ (5½, 5¾, 6, 6, 6½)"
14 (14, 14.5, 15, 15, 16.5) cm

sleeve

11¼ (12¼, 12¾, 13½, 15, 16)"
28.5 (31, 32.5, 34.5, 38, 40.5) cm

18 (18, 18½, 18½, 18½, 18¾)"
45.5 (45.5, 47, 47, 47, 47.5) cm

9 (10, 10, 10¾, 11¾, 11¾)"
23 (25.5, 25.5, 27.5, 30, 30) cm

INC ROW: (RS) K1, M1 (see Techniques), work to last st, M1, k1—2 sts inc'd.

Cont in St st, rep the inc row every 14 (18, 16, 16, 12, 10) rows 4 (4, 5, 5, 6, 8) more times, working new sts in St st—48 (52, 54, 58, 64, 68) sts. Work even until piece measures 18 (18, 18½, 18½, 18½, 18¾)" (45.5 [45.5, 47, 47, 47, 47.5] cm) from CO, ending with a WS row.

### Shape Sleeve Cap

BO 4 (5, 6, 6, 7, 9) sts at beg of next 2 rows—40 (42, 42, 46, 50, 50) sts. Dec 1 st at each side every RS row 2 (2, 2, 2, 3, 3) times, then every 4 rows 4 (4, 5, 5, 3, 4) times, then every RS row 4 (3, 3, 3, 6, 6) times, then every row 1 (3, 1, 3, 3, 2) time(s)—18 (18, 20, 20, 20, 20) sts rem. BO 3 sts at the beginning of the next 2 rows—12 (12, 14, 14, 14, 14) sts. BO rem sts.

# finishing

Block pieces to measurements. With yarn threaded on a tapestry needle, sew shoulder seams. Sew sleeves into armholes. Sew sleeve and side seams.

### Neckband

With shorter cir needle in smaller size and RS facing, pick up and knit 104 (112, 112, 120, 120, 120) sts around neck opening. Pm and join for working in rnds.

NEXT RND: *K2, p2; rep from *.

Rep the last rnd 6 more times. BO all sts in rib patt.

Weave in all loose ends.

# chapter 2

## URBAN BOHEMIA

On the weekend, city life slows down just enough to be able to enjoy some of the finer things. When I walk out of my office on Friday afternoon, my thoughts turn toward the long and leisurely hours to be spent checking out the hubs of activity and artistic happenings all over the city.

Among the things to choose from: stopping by one of the many greenmarkets to pick up some fresh veggies for a home-cooked meal; hanging out in the local coffee shop, nibbling on fresh-baked goodies while working on a crossword puzzle; visiting an art gallery in SoHo; taking in a spoken word performance at a café in Brooklyn; discovering a new restaurant in Astoria; strolling around the neighborhood at a snail's pace with nowhere to go and not a care in the world. The possibilities truly are endless.

The designs in this chapter are cozy, relaxed, and texture heavy: ideal for a more relaxed weekend look without compromising style. These are projects that are perfect for soft, gorgeous, natural fibers—what you throw on when you don't want to think about what to wear, but you still want to look and feel good.

# bleecker street
## CARDIGAN

**FINISHED SIZE**
32 (34½, 36½, 39, 42½, 46, 50½)" (81.5 [87.5, 92.5, 99, 108, 117, 128.5] cm) bust circumference, buttoned. Cardigan shown measures 34½" (87.5 cm).

**YARN**
Sportweight (#2 Fine).

**SHOWN HERE:** Brown Sheep *Lanaloft Sport* (100% wool; 145 yd [132 m]/50 g): #LL36 dark ash, 8 (9, 10, 11, 12, 13, 14) skeins.

**NEEDLES**
**BODY AND SLEEVES**—size U.S. 6 (4 mm): 24" (61 cm) circular (cir) needle.

*Adjust needle size, if necessary, to obtain the correct gauge.*

**NOTIONS**
Markers (m); stitch holders; tapestry needle; six contrasting ⅝" (16 mm) buttons, sewing needle and thread to match buttons.

**GAUGE**
21 sts and 28 rows = 4" (10 cm) in St st.

23 sts and 31 rows = 4" (10 cm) in texture st.

Simon and Garfunkel sang about a foggy café morning on Bleecker Street, and this cardigan is perfect for it—but has enough lively details to make it cheerful! Texture stitches, an A-line shape, and patch pockets all add interest. This raglan cardigan is not knit in one piece—the body and sleeves are in different stitch patterns with different row gauges, which makes it necessary to work the pieces separately and seam them together. But don't worry, the sewing will not be in vain. I added an exposed seam detail along the raglan lines to make it worth your while.

## stitch guide

### K1, P1, RIB
*(even number of sts)*

ALL ROWS: *K1, p1; rep from *.

Rep this row for patt.

### K1, P1, RIB
(odd number of sts)

ROW 1: (RS) K1, *p1, k1; rep from *.

ROW 2: (WS) P1, *k1, p1; rep from *.

Rep Rows 1 and 2 for patt.

### TEXTURE STITCH
*(odd number of sts)*

ROW 1: (RS) Knit.

ROW 2: (WS) Purl.

ROW 3: *K1, p1; rep from * to last st, k1.

ROW 4: Purl.

ROW 5: Knit.

ROW 6: *P1, k1; rep from * to last st, p1.

Rep Rows 1–6 for patt.

### 3-ROW BUTTONHOLE

ROW 1: (RS) K1, p1, k1, yarnover twice to make a double yo, k2tog, work to end.

ROW 2: (WS) Work in patt to double yo of previous row, work [k1, p1] in double yo, p1, k1, p1.

ROW 3: K1, p1, k1, work k2tog in [k1, p1] of previous row, work to end.

## notes

⊖ The front bands are worked at the same time as the body. After completing the fronts, the stitches for the bands are placed on holders to work later for the neckband.

⊖ Yarnover increases are worked above the waist on the right and left front only, creating a line of decorative eyelets.

## back

CO 108 (115, 120, 126, 136, 145, 157) sts. Work k1, p1 rib (see Stitch Guide) until piece measures 1" (2.5 cm), ending with a WS row.

NEXT ROW: (RS) K7 (5, 7, 3, 9, 7, 6) [k2tog, k5 (6, 6, 7, 7, 8, 9)] 13 times, k2tog, k8 (4, 7, 4, 8, 6, 6) sts—94 (101, 106, 112, 122, 131, 143) sts.

Change to St st. Place dart markers (m) as foll:

NEXT ROW: (WS) P23 (25, 26, 28, 30, 32, 35), place marker (pm) for dart, p48 (51, 54, 56, 62, 67, 73), pm dart, p23 (25, 26, 28, 30, 32, 35).

Slipping m (sl m) as you come to them, work even in St st until piece measures 4¼" (11 cm) from CO, ending with a WS row.

### Shape Waist

DEC ROW: (RS) Knit to first dart m, sl m, ssk (see Techniques), work to 2 sts before next dart m, k2tog, sl m, knit to end—2 sts dec'd.

Cont in St st, rep the dec row every 6 rows 8 (8, 8, 7, 7, 7, 6) more times, then every 8 rows 0 (0, 0, 1, 1, 1, 2) time(s)—76 (83, 88, 94, 104, 113, 125) sts; piece measures about 11¼ (11¼, 11¼, 11½, 11½, 11½, 11¾)" (28.5 [28.5, 28.5, 29, 29, 29, 30] cm) from CO. Work 7 rows even, beg and ending with a WS row.

INC ROW: (RS) Knit to dart m, sl m, M1 (see Techniques), knit to next dart m, M1, sl m, knit to end—2 sts inc'd.

Cont in St st, rep the inc row every 6 rows 3 more times—84 (91, 96, 102, 112, 121, 133) sts. Work even until piece measures 17 (17, 17, 17½, 17½, 17½, 18)" (43 [43, 43, 44.5, 44.5, 44.5, 45.5] cm) from beg, ending with a WS row.

### Shape Armholes

BO 6 (6, 7, 8, 9, 10, 13) sts at beg of next 2 rows—72 (79, 82, 86, 94, 101, 107) sts. Dec 1 st at each edge every RS row 16 (20, 21, 24, 27, 29, 31) times, then every 4 rows 4 (2, 2, 1, 0, 0, 0) times—32 (35, 36, 36, 40, 43, 45) sts rem; armholes measure 7¼ (7¼, 7½, 7¾, 8, 8½, 9¼)" (18.5 [18.5, 19, 19.5, 20.5, 21.5, 23.5] cm). BO all sts.

# right front

**note:** *The buttonholes are worked at the same time as the following instructions. Work the first 3-row buttonhole (see Stitch Guide) beginning on the 7 (7, 9, 11, 11, 9, 5)th row after the CO. After working the first 3-row buttonhole, *work 15 rows even between buttonholes, then work the next 3-row buttonhole; and repeat from * 4 more times for a total of 6 buttonholes. Count rows frequently to make sure you do not accidentally work past the point where a buttonhole should be made.*

CO 56 (59, 64, 68, 72, 77, 82) sts. Work k1, p1 rib until piece measures 1" (2.5 cm), ending with a WS row.

**NEXT ROW:** (RS) [K1, p1] 4 times for right front edge, pm, k8 (7, 9, 9, 11, 11, 11), [k2tog, k4 (5, 5, 5, 6, 6, 7, 8)] 5 times, k2tog, k8 (7, 10, 9, 11, 11, 11)—50 (53, 58, 62, 66, 71, 76) sts.

**NEXT ROW:** (WS) P23 (25, 26, 28, 30, 32, 35), pm for dart, p19 (20, 24, 26, 28, 31, 33), sl m, work 8 front edge sts in rib patt.

Keeping 8 marked sts at front edge (beg of RS rows, end of WS rows) in rib patt as established, work rem sts in St st. Work even until piece measures 4¼" (11 cm) from CO, ending with a WS row.

## Shape Waist

**DEC ROW:** (RS) Work 8 front edge sts, sl m, knit to 2 sts before dart m, k2tog, sl m, knit to end—1 st dec'd.

Cont in St st, rep the dec row every 6 rows 8 (8, 8, 7, 7, 7, 6) more times, then every 8 rows 0 (0, 0, 1, 1, 1, 2) time(s)—41 (44, 49, 53, 57, 62, 67) sts; piece measures about 11¼ (11¼, 11¼, 11½, 11½, 11½, 11¾)" (28.5 [28.5, 28.5, 29, 29, 29, 30] cm) from CO. Work 7 rows even, beg and ending with a WS row.

**INC ROW:** (RS) Work 8 front edge sts, sl m, knit to dart m, yo, sl m, knit to end—1 st inc'd.

Cont in St st, rep the inc row every 6 rows 3 more times, working new sts in St st—45 (48, 53, 57, 61, 66, 71) sts. Work even until piece measures 15½ (15½, 15¾, 16½, 16½, 17, 17¾)" (39.5 [39.5, 40, 42, 42, 43, 45] cm) from beg, ending with a WS row.

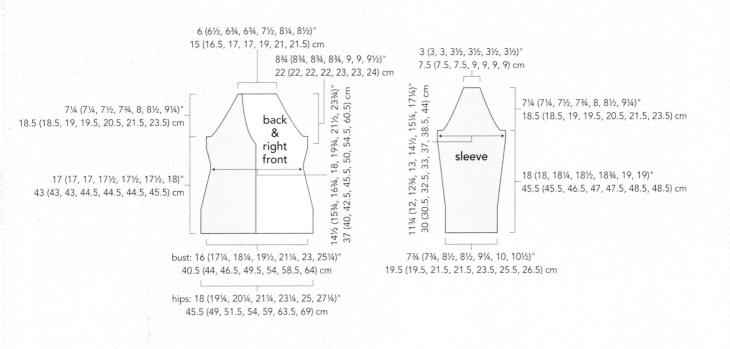

6 (6½, 6¾, 6¾, 7½, 8¼, 8½)"
15 (16.5, 17, 17, 19, 21, 21.5) cm

8¾ (8¾, 8¾, 8¾, 9, 9, 9½)"
22 (22, 22, 22, 23, 23, 24) cm

7¼ (7¼, 7½, 7¾, 8, 8½, 9¼)"
18.5 (18.5, 19, 19.5, 20.5, 21.5, 23.5) cm

back & right front

17 (17, 17, 17½, 17½, 17½, 18)"
43 (43, 43, 44.5, 44.5, 44.5, 45.5) cm

14½ (15¾, 16¾, 18, 19¾, 21½, 23¾)"
37 (40, 42.5, 45.5, 50, 54.5, 60.5) cm

bust: 16 (17¼, 18¼, 19½, 21¼, 23, 25¼)"
40.5 (44, 46.5, 49.5, 54, 58.5, 64) cm

hips: 18 (19¼, 20¼, 21¼, 23¼, 25, 27¼)"
45.5 (49, 51.5, 54, 59, 63.5, 69) cm

3 (3, 3, 3½, 3½, 3½, 3½)"
7.5 (7.5, 7.5, 9, 9, 9, 9) cm

7¼ (7¼, 7½, 7¾, 8, 8½, 9¼)"
18.5 (18.5, 19, 19.5, 20.5, 21.5, 23.5) cm

11¾ (12, 12¾, 13, 14½, 15¼, 17¼)"
30 (30.5, 32.5, 33, 37, 38.5, 44) cm

sleeve

18 (18, 18¼, 18½, 18¾, 19, 19)"
45.5 (45.5, 46.5, 47, 47.5, 48.5, 48.5) cm

7¾ (7¾, 8½, 8½, 9¼, 10, 10½)"
19.5 (19.5, 21.5, 21.5, 23.5, 25.5, 26.5) cm

## Shape Front Neck and Armhole

**note:** *The armhole shaping is introduced while the front neck shaping is in progress; read the next sections all the way through before proceeding.*

NECK DEC ROW: (RS) Work 8 front edge sts, sl m, k1, ssk, work to end—1 st dec'd.

For neck shaping, rep the neck dec row every 2 rows 0 (0, 4, 5, 7, 10, 9) times, then every 4 rows 6 (9, 10, 10, 9, 8, 9) times, then every 6 rows 4 (2, 0, 0, 0, 0, 0) times—11 (12, 15, 16, 17, 19, 19) sts total removed from neck edge, including first neck dec row.

*At the same time,* when piece measures 17 (17, 17, 17½, 17½, 17½, 18)" (43 [43, 43, 44.5, 44.5, 44.5, 45.5] cm) from beg, shape armhole by BO 6 (6, 7, 8, 9, 10, 13) sts at beg of next WS row, then dec 1 st at armhole edge (end of RS rows) every RS row 16 (20, 21, 24, 27, 29, 31) times, then every 4 rows 4 (2, 2, 1, 0, 0, 0) times—26 (28, 30, 33, 36, 39, 44) sts total removed by armhole shaping.

When all shaping has been completed—8 front edge sts rem; armhole measures 7¼ (7¼, 7½, 7¾, 8, 8½, 9¼)" (18.5 [18.5, 19, 19.5, 20.5, 21.5, 23.5] cm). Place rem sts on holder and break yarn.

## left front

CO 56 (59, 64, 68, 72, 77, 82) sts. Work k1, p1 rib until piece measures 1" (2.5 cm), ending with a WS row.

NEXT ROW: (RS) K8 (7, 10, 9, 11, 11, 11), k2tog, [k4 (5, 5, 6, 6, 7, 8), k2tog] 5 times, k8 (7, 9, 9, 11, 11, 11), pm, [p1, k1] 4 times for left front edge.

NEXT ROW: (WS) Work 8 front edge sts in patt, sl m, p19 (20, 24, 26, 28, 31, 33), pm for dart, p23 (25, 26, 28, 30, 32, 35).

Keeping 8 marked sts at front edge (end of RS rows, beg of WS rows) in rib patt as established, work rem sts in St st. Work even until piece measures 4¼" (11 cm) from CO, ending with a WS row.

## Shape Waist

**DEC ROW:** (RS) Knit to dart m, sl m, ssk, knit to last 8 sts, sl m, work 8 front edge sts—1 st dec'd.

Cont in St st, rep the dec row every 6 rows 8 (8, 8, 7, 7, 7, 6) more times, then every 8 rows 0 (0, 0, 1, 1, 1, 2) time(s)—41 (44, 49, 53, 57, 62, 67) sts; piece measures about 11¼ (11¼, 11¼, 11½, 11½, 11½, 11¾)" (28.5 [28.5, 28.5, 29, 29, 29, 30] cm) from CO. Work 7 rows even, beg and ending with a WS row.

**INC ROW:** (RS) Knit to dart m, sl m, yo, knit to last 8 sts, sl m, work 8 front edge sts—1 st inc'd.

Cont in St st, rep the inc row every 6 rows 3 more times, working new sts in St st—45 (48, 53, 57, 61, 66, 71) sts. Work even until piece measures 15½ (15½, 15¾, 16½, 16½, 17, 17¾)" (39.5 [39.5, 40, 42, 42, 43, 45] cm) from beg, ending with a WS row.

## Shape Front Neck and Armhole

**note:** *As for the right front, the armhole shaping begins while the neck shaping is in progress; read the next sections all the way through before proceeding.*

**NECK DEC ROW:** (RS) Work to last 11 sts, k2tog, k1, sl m, work 8 front edge sts—1 st dec'd.

For neck shaping, rep the neck dec row every 2 rows 0 (0, 4, 5, 7, 10, 9) times, then every 4 rows 6 (9, 10, 10, 9, 8, 9) times, then every 6 rows 4 (2, 0, 0, 0, 0, 0) times—11 (12, 15, 16, 17, 19, 19) sts total removed from neck edge, including first neck dec row.

*At the same time,* when piece measures 17 (17, 17, 17½, 17½, 17½, 18)" (43 [43, 43, 44.5, 44.5, 44.5, 45.5] cm) from beg, shape armhole by BO 6 (6, 7, 8, 9, 10, 13) sts at beg of next RS row, then dec 1 st at armhole edge (beg of RS rows) every RS row 16 (20, 21, 24, 27, 29, 31) times, then every 4 rows 4 (2, 2, 1, 0, 0, 0) times—26 (28, 30, 33, 36, 39, 44) sts total removed by armhole shaping.

When all shaping has been completed—8 front edge sts rem; armhole measures 7¼ (7¼, 7½, 7¾, 8, 8½, 9¼)" (18.5 [18.5, 19, 19.5, 20.5, 21.5, 23.5] cm). Place rem sts on holder and break yarn.

## sleeves

CO 45 (45, 49, 49, 53, 57, 61) sts. Work k1, p1 rib until piece measures 2½" (6.5 cm), ending with a WS row.

Change to textured st patt (see Stitch Guide), and work even until sleeve measures 4½" (11.5 cm) from CO, ending with a WS row.

**INC ROW:** (RS) K1, M1, work in patt to last st, M1, k1—2 sts inc'd.

Cont in patt, rep the inc row every 8 (8, 8, 6, 6, 6, 4) rows 5 (10, 9, 1, 8, 10, 5) more time(s), then every 10 (10, 10, 8, 8, 8, 6) rows 5 (1, 2, 11, 6, 4, 13) time(s), working new sts into established patt—67 (69, 73, 75, 83, 87, 99) sts. Work even in patt until sleeve measures 18 (18, 18¼, 18½, 18¾, 19, 19)" (45.5 [45.5, 46.5, 47, 47.5, 48.5, 48.5] cm), ending with a WS row.

## Shape Sleeve Cap

BO 6 (6, 7, 8, 9, 10, 13) sts at beg of next 2 rows—55 (57, 59, 59, 65, 67, 73) sts rem. Dec 1 st each end of needle every RS row 11 (13, 14, 9, 14, 14, 17) times, then every 4 rows 8 (7, 7, 10, 8, 9, 9) times—17 (17, 17, 21, 21, 21, 21) sts rem. BO all sts.

# finishing

Block pieces to measurements. With yarn threaded on a tapestry needle, sew raglan seams using mattress stitch (see Techniques), and working from the WS so the 1-st seam allowance shows on the RS of the garment. Sew sleeve and side seams.

## Neckband

Return 8 held right front sts to needle and rejoin yarn with WS facing.

NEXT ROW: (WS) K1f&b (see Techniques), work in established rib to end—9 sts.

Working new st in St st, work even in established rib until piece reaches across top of right sleeve to right back raglan seam when slightly stretched. Place sts on holder. Return 8 held left front sts to needle and rejoin yarn with RS facing.

NEXT ROW: (RS) K1f&b, work in established rib to end—9 sts.

Working new st in St st, work even in established rib until piece reaches across top of left sleeve and along back neck to right back raglan seam when slightly stretched. Return 9 held sts of right front band to needle and use Kitchener st (see Techniques) or the three-needle bind-off method (see Techniques) to join ends of bands. With yarn threaded on a tapestry needle, sew selvedge of band to top of sleeves and back neck.

## Pockets (make 2)

CO 43 (43, 43, 45, 47, 49, 51) sts. Work in texture st until piece measures 5½ (5½, 5½, 5½, 5¾, 5¾, 6)" (14 [14, 14, 14, 14.5, 14.5, 15] cm), ending with a WS row. Work 4 rows in k1, p1 rib. BO all sts in rib patt. Sew each pocket to RS of garment with lower edge of pocket 1½" (3.8 cm) up from CO edge of sweater and centered over the side seam.

Weave in all loose ends. Using sewing needle and thread, sew buttons to left front, opposite buttonholes.

# magnolia café

## CARDIGAN

### FINISHED SIZE

36½ (38½, 40½, 43½, 48, 52½)" (92.5 [98, 103, 110.5, 122, 133.5] cm) bust circumference, buttoned. Cardigan shown measures 36½" (92.5 cm).

### YARN

Worsted Weight (#4 Medium).

**SHOWN HERE:** O-Wool *Classic Worsted* (100% certified organic merino; 99 yd [90 m]/50 g): #7100 oatmeal (MC), 12 (13, 14, 15, 16, 17) skeins; #4411 begonia (CC), 1 skein for all sizes.

### NEEDLES

**BODY AND SLEEVES**—size U.S. 9 (5.5 mm): 24" (61 cm) circular (cir) needle.

**RIBBING**—size U.S. 8 (5 mm): 24" (61 cm) cir needle.

*Adjust needle sizes, if necessary, to obtain the correct gauge.*

### NOTIONS

Markers (m); cable needle (cn); stitch holders; tapestry needle; six 1" (2.5 cm) buttons.

### GAUGE

15 sts and 20 rows = 4" (10 cm) in double moss st on larger needle.

16 sts and 20 rows = 4" (10 cm) in rev St st (purl on RS rows, knit on WS rows) on larger needle.

24 sts of Cable chart measure 3¾" (9.5 cm) wide on larger needle.

4 sts of right and left rope cable patts measure 1" (2.5 cm) wide on larger needle.

This one is as sweet as a cupcake from its namesake bakery! Cabled cardigans with a shawl collar are one of the most classic, timeless styles you could ever knit for yourself. I brought this one up-to-date with contrasting pocket linings and little touches of color, including using contrasting color yarn to sew on the buttons—feel free to get creative with your own color combinations. Instead of using an all-over cable pattern, which can be a bit overwhelming in a heavier yarn, I used double moss stitch for the back and sleeves to add a different texture.

## stitch guide

### 2/2 RC
Sl 2 sts onto cable needle (cn) and hold in back, k2, k2 from cn.

### 2/2 LC
Sl 2 sts onto cn and hold in front, k2, k2 from cn.

### K2, P2 RIB
**(multiple of 4 sts + 2)**

ROW 1: (RS) K2, *p2, k2; rep from * to end.

ROW 2: (WS) P2, *k2, p2; rep from * to end.

Rep Rows 1 and 2 for patt.

### DOUBLE MOSS STITCH
**(even number of sts)**

ROW 1: (RS) *K1, p1; rep from * to end.

ROW 2: (WS) *P1, k1; rep from * to end.

ROW 3: *P1, k1; rep from * to end.

ROW 4: *K1, p1; rep from * to end.

Rep Rows 1–4 for patt.

### RIGHT ROPE CABLE
**(worked on 4 sts)**

ROW 1: (RS) 2/2 RC (see Stitch Guide).

ROWS 2 AND 4: (WS) P4.

ROWS 3 AND 5: K4.

ROW 6: P4.

Rep Rows 1–6 for patt.

### LEFT ROPE CABLE
**(worked on 4 sts)**

ROW 1: (RS) 2/2 LC (see Stitch Guide).

ROWS 2 AND 4: (WS) P4.

ROWS 3 AND 5: K4.

ROW 6: P4.

Rep Rows 1–6 for patt.

## notes

- During shaping, if there are not enough stitches to work a complete cable, work the stitches of the partial cable in stockinette.

- The front bands and shawl collar are worked in two mirror-image pieces that are seamed together at the center back neck, then sewn to the front edges of the cardigan. I find that the bind-off edge of a shawl collar can sometimes look untidy, so I have chosen not to pick up stitches for the bands and collar along the edges of the garment. Instead, the bind-off edge of the assembled collar and bands is sewn to the body, leaving the cast-on edge showing (which looks much nicer).

- When choosing buttons, make sure they have holes large enough to fit a tapestry needle threaded with a strand of the contrasting color (CC) yarn.

## pocket lining (make 2)

With larger needle and CC, CO 26 sts. Work in St st for 4" (10 cm), ending with a RS row. Change to MC. Work 2 rows in St st, BO 1 st at beg of each row—24 sts rem. Work Rows 2 and 3 of Cable chart, ending with a RS row. Place sts on holder and break yarn. Make a second pocket lining in the same manner.

## back

With MC yarn and smaller needle, CO 70 (74, 78, 86, 94, 102) sts. Work k2, p2 rib (see Stitch Guide) until piece measures 2" (5 cm), ending with a WS row. Change to larger needle. Work in double moss st (see Stitch Guide) until piece measures 4½" (11.5 cm) from CO, ending with a WS row.

### Shape Waist

DEC ROW: (RS) K1, ssk (see Techniques), work in patt to last 3 sts, k2tog, k1—2 sts dec'd.

Cont in patt, rep the dec row every 6 rows 2 (2, 1, 5, 5, 5) more time(s), then every 8 rows 2 (2, 3, 0, 0, 0) times—60 (64, 68, 74, 82, 90) sts; piece measures about 10¼ (10¼, 10¾, 10¾, 10¾, 10¾)" (26 [26, 27.5, 27.5, 27.5, 27.5] cm) from CO. Work even for 7 rows, beg and ending with a WS row.

INC ROW: (RS) K1, M1 (see Techniques), work to last st, M1, k1—2 sts inc'd.

Cont in patt, rep the inc row every 8 rows 3 times, working new sts into established patt—68 (72, 76, 82, 90, 98) sts. Work even until back measures 17¾ (17¾, 18, 18, 18¼, 18¼)" (45 [45, 45.5, 45.5, 46.5, 46.5] cm) from CO, ending with a WS row.

### Shape Armholes

BO 4 (4, 4, 5, 7, 8) sts at beg of next 2 rows—60 (64, 68, 72, 76, 82) sts. Dec 1 st each side every row 4 (4, 5, 6, 7, 8) times—52 (56, 58, 60, 62, 66) sts rem. Cont in patt until armholes measure 7 (7¼, 7½, 7¾, 8, 8½)" (18 [18.5, 19, 19.5, 20.5, 21.5] cm), ending with a WS row.

### Shape Back Neck

NEXT ROW: (RS) Work 13 (13, 14, 14, 15, 17) sts, join second ball of yarn and BO center 26 (30,

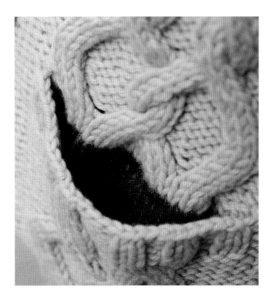

30, 32, 32, 32) sts for back neck, work in patt to end—13 (13, 14, 14, 15, 17) sts rem each side. Working each side separately, dec 1 st at each neck edge on the next 2 rows—11 (11, 12, 12, 13, 15) sts rem each side; armholes measure about 7½ (7¾, 8, 8¼, 8½, 9)" (19 [19.5, 20.5, 21, 21.5, 23] cm).

### Shape Shoulders

At each armhole edge, BO 5 (5, 6, 6, 6, 7) sts once, then 6 (6, 6, 6, 7, 8) sts once—no sts rem.

## right front

With MC yarn and smaller needle, CO 31 (35, 35, 39, 43, 47) sts.

NEXT ROW: (RS) K1, (edge st), work Row 1 of k2, p2 rib over 30 (34, 34, 38, 42, 46) sts.

Keeping edge st in St st, work in k2, p2 rib until piece measures 2" (5 cm), ending with a WS row, and dec 0 (dec 1, inc 1, inc 1, inc 1, inc 1) st in last row—31 (34, 36, 40, 44, 48) sts. Change to larger needle.

NEXT ROW: (RS) K1 (edge st), M1, k2, M1, place marker (pm), p3 (3, 4, 4, 5, 6), M1P (see Techniques), p2 (3, 3, 4, 5, 6), pm, p3, M1P, [k1, M1] 3 times, p3, M1P, [k1, M1] 3 times, p3, M1P, pm, p2 (3, 4, 4, 5, 6), M1P, p3 (4, 4, 5, 6, 7), k3 (3, 3, 5, 5, 5)—44 (47, 49, 53, 57, 61) sts.

NEXT ROW: (WS) P3 (3, 3, 5, 5, 5) for St st, k6 (8, 9, 10, 12, 14) for rev St st, slip marker (sl m), [k4, p6] 2 times, k4, sl m, k6 (7, 8, 9, 11, 13) for rev St st, sl m, p5.

NEXT ROW: (RS) K1 (edge st), work Row 1 of left rope cable (see Stitch Guide) over 4 sts, work 6 (7, 8, 9, 11, 13) rev St sts, sl m, work Row 1 of Cable chart over 24 sts, sl m, work 6 (8, 9, 10, 12, 14) rev St sts, work 3 (3, 3, 5, 5, 5) St sts (side sts).

## Shape Waist and Insert Pocket

**note:** *The pocket insertion is worked while the waist shaping is in progress; read the next sections all the way through before proceeding.*

For waist shaping, when piece measures 4½" (11.5 cm) from CO dec 1 st at side by working last 5 sts as k2tog, k3 starting on the next RS row, then every 6 rows 2 (2, 1, 5, 5, 5) more time(s), then every 8 rows 2 (2, 3, 0, 0, 0) times—5 (5, 5, 6, 6, 6) sts total removed by waist shaping.

*At the same time,* for pocket work sts in established patts, including any waist shaping, until Row 22 of Cable chart has been completed, then work Rows 1 and 2 once more.

NEXT ROW: (RS) Work in patt to marked Cable chart sts, sl m, [k2, p2] 2 times, k2, p4, k2, [p2, k2] 2 times, sl m, work in patt to end.

Work 3 rows in patt, including any waist shaping, and working 24 sts between m as they appear (knit the knits and purl the purls) for pocket welt.

NEXT ROW: (RS) Work in patt to marked pocket sts, sl m, BO 24 sts, sl m, work to end.

NEXT ROW: (WS) Work in patt to BO gap of previous row, sl m, place 24 held pocket lining sts on left needle with WS facing, work Row 4 of Cable chart over lining sts, sl m, work in patt to end.

Cont in patt until all waist dec's have been completed—39 (42, 44, 47, 51, 55) sts rem; piece measures about 10¼ (10¼, 10¾, 10¾, 10¾, 10¾)" (26 [26, 27.5, 27.5, 27.5, 27.5] cm) from CO. Work even for 7 rows, beg and ending with a WS row.

INC ROW: (RS) Work in patt to last 3 sts, M1, k3—1 st inc'd.

Cont in patt, rep the inc row every 8 rows 3 times, working new sts into established patt—

43 (46, 48, 51, 55, 59) sts. Work even until piece measures 17 (17¼, 17½, 17½, 17¾, 17¾)" (43 [44, 44.5, 44.5, 45, 45] cm) from CO, ending with a WS row.

## Shape Front Neck and Armhole

**note:** *The neck shaping will be in progress when the armhole shaping is introduced; read the next sections all the way through before proceeding.*

RS NECK DEC ROW: (RS) K1 (edge st), work 4 sts rope cable, sl m, p1, p2tog, work in patt to end—1 st dec'd.

WS NECK DEC ROW: (WS) Work in patt to last 8 sts, k2tog, k1, sl m, work 4 sts rope cable, p1 (edge st)—1 st dec'd.

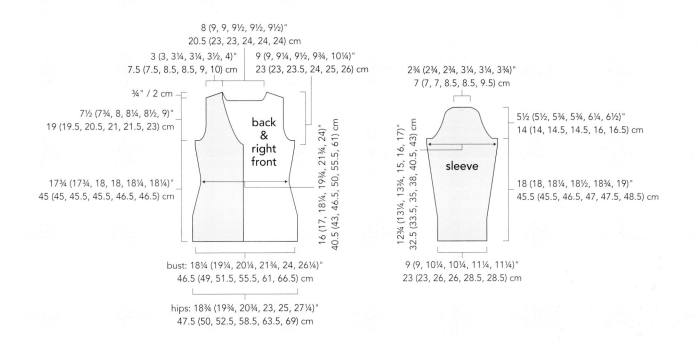

For neck shaping, dec 1 st at neck edge inside rope cable as above on the next 7 (11, 11, 11, 10, 10) rows, then every RS row 15 (13, 13, 14, 15, 16) times—24 (26, 26, 27, 27, 28) sts total removed at neck edge, including first 2 neck dec rows.

*At the same time,* when piece measures 17¾ (17¾, 18, 18, 18¼, 18¼)" (45 [45, 45.5, 45.5, 46.5, 46.5] cm) from CO, shape armhole by BO 4 (4, 4, 5, 7, 8) sts at beg of next WS row, then dec 1 st at armhole edge (end of RS rows, beg of WS rows) every row 4 (5, 6, 7, 8, 8) times—8 (9, 10, 12, 15, 16) sts total removed at armhole edge.

When all neck and armhole shaping have been completed—11 (11, 12, 12, 13, 15) sts rem. Work even in established patts until armhole measures 7½ (7¾, 8, 8¼, 8½, 9)" (19 [19.5, 20.5, 21, 21.5, 23] cm), ending with a RS row.

## Shape Shoulder

BO 5 (5, 6, 6, 6, 7) sts at beg of next WS row, then 6 (6, 6, 6, 7, 8) sts at beg of foll WS row—no sts rem.

# left front

With MC yarn and smaller needle, CO 31 (35, 35, 39, 43, 47) sts.

NEXT ROW: (RS) Work Row 1 of k2, p2 rib over 30 (34, 34, 38, 42, 46) sts, k1 (edge st).

Keeping edge st in St st, work in k2, p2 rib until piece measures 2" (5 cm), ending with a WS row, and dec 0 (dec 1, inc 1, inc 1, inc 1, inc 1) st in last row—31 (34, 36, 40, 44, 48) sts. Change to larger needle.

NEXT ROW: (RS) K3 (3, 3, 5, 5, 5), p3 (4, 4, 5, 6, 7), M1P, p2 (3, 4, 4, 5, 6), pm, M1P, p3, [M1, k1] 3 times, M1P, p3, [M1, k1] 3 times, M1P, p3, pm, p2 (3, 3, 4, 5, 6), M1P, p3 (3, 4, 4, 5, 6), pm, M1, k2, M1, k1 (edge st)—44 (47, 49, 53, 57, 61) sts.

NEXT ROW: (WS) P5, sl m, k6 (7, 8, 9, 11, 13) for rev St st, sl m, k4, [p6, k4] 2 times, sl m, k6 (8, 9, 10, 12, 14) for rev St st, p3 (3, 3, 5, 5, 5) for St st.

NEXT ROW: (RS) Work 3 (3, 3, 5, 5, 5) St sts (side sts), work 6 (8, 9, 10, 12, 14) rev St sts, sl m, work Row 1 of Cable chart over 24 sts, sl m, work 6 (7,

8, 9, 11, 13) rev St sts, work Row 1 of right rope cable (see Stitch Guide) over 4 sts, k1 (edge st).

## Shape Waist and Insert Pocket

**note:** *As for the right front, the pocket insertion is worked while the waist shaping is in progress. Read the next sections all the way through before proceeding.*

For waist shaping, when piece measures 4½" (11.5 cm) from CO dec 1 st at side by working first 5 sts as k3, ssk (see Techniques) starting on the next RS row, then every 6 rows 2 (2, 1, 5, 5, 5) more time(s), then every 8 rows 2 (2, 3, 0, 0, 0) times—5 (5, 5, 6, 6, 6) sts total removed by waist shaping.

*At the same time,* for pocket, work sts in established patts including any waist shaping until Row 22 of Cable chart has been completed, then work Rows 1 and 2 once more.

**NEXT ROW:** (RS) Work in patt to marked Cable chart sts, sl m, [k2, p2] 2 times, k2, p4, k2, [p2, k2] 2 times, sl m, work in patt to end.

Work 3 rows in patt, including any waist shaping, and working 24 sts between m as they appear (knit the knits and purl the purls) for pocket welt.

**NEXT ROW:** (RS) Work in patt to marked pocket sts, sl m, BO 24 sts, sl m, work to end.

**NEXT ROW:** (WS) Work in patt to BO gap of previous row, sl m, place 24 held pocket lining

sts on left needle with WS facing, work Row 4 of Cable chart over lining sts, sl m, work in patt to end.

Cont in patt until all waist dec's have been completed—39 (42, 44, 47, 51, 55) sts rem; piece measures about 10¼ (10¼, 10¾, 10¾, 10¾, 10¾)" (26 [26, 27.5, 27.5, 27.5, 27.5] cm) from CO. Work even for 7 rows, beg and ending with a WS row.

**INC ROW:** (RS) K3, M1, work in patt to end—1 st inc'd.

Cont in patt, rep the inc row every 8 rows 3 times, working new sts into established patt—43 (46, 48, 51, 55, 59) sts. Work even until piece measures 17 (17¼, 17½, 17½, 17¾, 17¾)" (43 [44, 44.5, 44.5, 45, 45] cm) from CO, ending with a WS row.

## Shape Front Neck and Armhole

**note:** *As for the right front, the neck shaping will be in progress when the armhole shaping is introduced; read the next sections all the way through before proceeding.*

**RS NECK DEC ROW:** (RS) Work in patt to last 8 sts, ssp (see Techniques), p1, sl m, work 4 sts rope cable, k1 (edge st)—1 st dec'd.

**WS NECK DEC ROW:** (WS) P1 (edge st), work 4 sts rope cable, sl m, k1, ssk, work in patt to end—1 st dec'd.

---

| | knit on RS; purl on WS |
| | purl on RS; knit on WS |
| | sl 1 st to cn and hold in back, k3, p1 from cn |
| | sl 3 sts to cn and hold in front, p1, k3 from cn |
| | sl 2 sts to cn and hold in back, k3, p2 from cn |
| | sl 3 sts to cn and hold in front, p2, k3 from cn |
| | sl 3 sts to cn and hold in back, k3, k3 from cn |
| | sl 3 sts to cn and hold in front, k3, k3 from cn |

### Cable

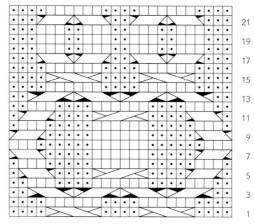

24 sts

For neck shaping, dec 1 st at neck edge inside rope cable as above on the next 7 (11, 11, 11, 10, 10) rows, then every RS row 15 (13, 13, 14, 15, 16) times—24 (26, 26, 27, 27, 28) sts total removed at neck edge, including first 2 neck dec rows.

*At the same time*, when piece measures 17¾ (17¾, 18, 18, 18¼, 18¼)" (45 [45, 45.5, 45.5, 46.5, 46.5] cm) from CO, shape armhole by BO 4 (4, 4, 5, 7, 8) sts at beg of next RS row, then dec 1 st at armhole edge (beg of RS rows, end of WS rows) every row 4 (5, 6, 7, 8, 8) times—8 (9, 10, 12, 15, 16) sts total removed at armhole edge.

When all neck and armhole shaping have been completed—11 (11, 12, 12, 13, 15) sts rem. Work even in established patts until armhole measures 7½ (7¾, 8, 8¼, 8½, 9)" (19 [19.5, 20.5, 21, 21.5, 23] cm), ending with a WS row.

## Shape Shoulder

BO 5 (5, 6, 6, 6, 7) sts at beg of next RS row, then 6 (6, 6, 6, 7, 8) sts at beg of foll RS row—no sts rem.

# sleeves

With MC and smaller needle, CO 34 (34, 38, 38, 42, 42) sts. Work in k2, p2 rib until piece measures 3" (7.5 cm). Change to larger needle. Work in double moss st until piece measures 4" (10 cm) from CO, ending with a WS row.

INC ROW: (RS) K1, M1, work to last st, M1, k1—2 sts inc'd.

Cont in patt, rep the inc row every 10 (8, 10, 8, 8, 6) rows 4 (3, 3, 6, 5, 4) more times, then every 12 (10, 12, 10, 10, 8) rows 2 (4, 3, 2, 3, 6) times, working new sts into patt—48 (50, 52, 56, 60, 64) sts. Work even in patt until sleeve measures 18 (18, 18¼, 18½, 18¾, 19)" (45.5 [45.5, 46.5, 47, 47.5, 48.5] cm) from CO, ending with a WS row.

## Shape Sleeve Cap

BO 4 (4, 4, 5, 7, 8) sts at beg of next 2 rows—40 (42, 44, 46, 46, 48) sts. Dec 1 st at each side every RS row 2 (4, 5, 5, 4, 3) times, then every 4 rows 3 (2, 2, 2, 3, 4) times, then every row 7 times—16 (16, 16, 18, 18, 20) sts rem. BO 3 sts at the beg of the next 2 rows—10 (10, 10, 12, 12, 14) sts. BO all sts.

# finishing

Block pieces to measurements. With MC threaded on a tapestry needle, sew shoulder seams. Sew sleeves into armholes. Sew sleeve and side seams. Sew pocket linings to WS of fronts as invisibly as possible using MC.

## Front Bands and Collar

### Buttonband and left collar

With MC yarn and smaller needle, CO 122 (126, 128, 132, 134, 136) sts.

**NEXT ROW:** (WS) P0 (0, 2, 2, 0, 2), work Row 2 of k2, p2 rib over 122 (126, 126, 130, 134, 134) sts.

Work as established for 8 more rows, ending with a WS row—piece measures about 1½" (3.8 cm).

**NEXT ROW:** (RS) BO 70 (74, 74, 74, 76, 76) sts, work to end—52 (52, 54, 58, 58, 60) sts.

**NEXT ROW:** (WS) Work even.

**NEXT ROW:** BO 3 sts, work to end.

Cont in patt, rep the shaping of the last 2 rows 7 (7, 9, 11, 11, 13) more times, ending with a RS row—28 (28, 24, 22, 22, 18) sts rem.

**NEXT ROW:** Work even.

**NEXT ROW:** BO 4 sts, work to end.

Cont in patt, rep the shaping of the last 2 rows 3 (3, 2, 1, 1, 0) more time(s), ending with a RS row—12 (12, 12, 14, 14, 14) sts. Work 1 WS row even—piece measures about 6 (6, 6¼, 6¾, 6¾, 7)" (15 [15, 16, 17, 17, 18] cm) at highest point. BO all sts in patt.

### Buttonhole band and right collar

With MC yarn and smaller needle, CO 122 (126, 128, 132, 134, 136) sts.

**NEXT ROW:** (WS) Work Row 2 of k2, p2 rib over 122 (126, 126, 130, 134, 134) sts, p0 (0, 2, 2, 0, 2).

Work as established for 4 more rows, ending with a WS row.

**BUTTONHOLE ROW:** (RS) Work 52 (52, 54, 58, 58, 60) sts in patt, [work a 5-st one-row buttonhole (see Techniques), work until there are 7 (8, 8, 8, 8, 8) sts on right needle after buttonhole] 5 times, work a 5-st one-row buttonhole, work in patt to end—6 buttonholes completed.

Work as established for 3 more rows, ending with a RS row—piece measures about 1½" (3.8 cm).

**NEXT ROW:** (WS) BO 70 (74, 74, 74, 76, 76) sts, work to end—52 (52, 54, 58, 58, 60) sts.

**NEXT ROW:** (RS) Work even.

**NEXT ROW:** BO 3 sts, work to end.

Cont in patt, rep the shaping of the last 2 rows 7 (7, 9, 11, 11, 13) more times, ending with a WS row—28 (28, 24, 22, 22, 18) sts rem.

**NEXT ROW:** Work even.

**NEXT ROW:** BO 4 sts, work to end.

Cont in patt, rep the shaping of the last 2 rows 3 (3, 2, 1, 1, 0) more time(s), ending with a WS row—12 (12, 12, 14, 14, 14) sts. Work 1 RS row even—piece measures about 6 (6, 6¼, 6¾, 6¾, 7)" (15 [15, 16, 17, 17, 18] cm) at highest point. BO all sts in patt.

Sew collar halves together at center back, reversing the seam so the seam allowance shows on the RS of the garment and will be concealed when the collar is folded back. Sew shaped BO edges of assembled collar and bands along front and back neck edges, making sure the buttonholes are on the right front, and centering the collar seam at back neck.

Weave in all loose ends. Using CC yarn threaded on a tapestry needle, sew buttons to buttonband, opposite buttonholes.

# washington square
## CARDIGAN

### FINISHED SIZE
36½ (39, 41, 44½, 50½)" (92.5 [99, 104, 113, 128.5] cm) bust circumference, buttoned. Cardigan shown measures 36½" (92.5 cm), buttoned.

### YARN
Chunky Weight (#5 Bulky).

**SHOWN HERE:** Cascade Yarns *Ecological Wool* (100% wool; 478 yd [437 m]/250 g): #8085 mocha, 2 (3, 3, 3, 4) skeins.

### NEEDLES
**BODY AND SLEEVES**—size U.S. 10 (6 mm): 24" (61 cm) circular (cir) needle.

**RIBBING**—size U.S. 9 (5.5 mm): straight.

*Adjust needle sizes, if necessary, to obtain the correct gauge.*

### NOTIONS
Markers (m); stitch holder; tapestry needle; seven 1" (2.5 cm) buttons; sewing needle and matching thread.

### GAUGE
14 sts and 20 rows = 4" (10 cm) in St st on larger needles.

When I first started designing handknits, chunky yarns weren't part of my repertoire. My view toward them wasn't very positive, but maybe that was because I hadn't found the right pattern. The key to working with heavier yarns is adding just enough positive ease for fit purposes without making the wearer look puffy. This cardigan has a nicely contoured shape with a simple lace panel up the front. I love working lace in chunky yarns because of the rustic look it creates, especially in a natural-colored wool.

## stitch guide

### K2, P2 RIB
*(multiple of 4 sts + 2)*

ROW 1: (WS) P2, *k2, p2; rep from *.

ROW 2: (RS) K2, *p2, k2; rep from *.

Rep Rows 1 and 2 for patt.

## back

With smaller needles, CO 74 (78, 82, 90, 98) sts. Work in k2, p2 rib (see Stitch Guide) for 2" (5 cm), beg and ending with a WS row. Change to larger cir needle and St st.

NEXT ROW: (RS) K3 (5, 7, 5, 4), [k2tog, k4 (4, 4, 4, 6)] 11 (11, 11, 13, 11) times, k2tog, k3 (5, 7, 5, 4)—62 (66, 70, 76, 86) sts.

NEXT ROW: (WS) Purl—piece measures about 2½" (6.5 cm) from CO.

### Shape Waist

DEC ROW: (RS) K1, ssk (see Techniques), knit to last 3 sts, k2tog, k1—2 sts dec'd.

Cont in St st, rep the dec row every 12 (12, 14, 14, 14) rows 2 more times—56 (60, 64, 70, 80) sts; piece measures about 7½ (7½, 8¼, 8¼, 8¼)" (19 [19, 21, 21, 21] cm) from CO. Work even in St st for 5 rows, beg and ending with a WS row.

INC ROW: (RS) K1, M1 (see Techniques), knit to last st, M1, k1—2 sts inc'd.

Cont in St st, rep the inc row every 8 rows 3 more times, working new sts in St st—64 (68, 72, 78, 88) sts. Work even until piece measures 15 (15, 15½, 15½, 16)" (38 [38, 39.5, 39.5, 40.5] cm) from CO, ending with a WS row.

### Shape Armholes

BO 4 (4, 4, 5, 7) sts at the beginning of the next 2 rows—56 (60, 64, 68, 74) sts. Dec 1 st at each armhole edge every row 3 (3, 4, 5, 6) times—50 (54, 56, 58, 62) sts. Work even until armholes measure 7¾ (8¼, 8¾, 9¼, 9½)" (19.5 [21, 22, 23.5, 24] cm), ending with a WS row.

### Shape Back Neck and Shoulders

NEXT ROW: (RS) BO 3 (3, 4, 4, 5) sts, knit until there are 7 (9, 9, 9, 10) sts on right needle after BO, place rem 40 (42, 43, 45, 47) sts on holder—7 (9, 9, 9, 10) right back shoulder sts rem on needle. Cont as foll:

### Right back shoulder

NEXT ROW: (WS) P2tog at neck edge, purl to end—6 (8, 8, 8, 9) sts.

NEXT ROW: (RS) BO 3 (3, 4, 4, 4) sts, knit to last 2 sts, k2tog—2 (4, 3, 3, 4) sts.

NEXT ROW: Purl.

BO all sts with RS facing.

### Left back shoulder

Return 40 (42, 43, 45, 47) held sts to needle and rejoin yarn with RS facing.

NEXT ROW: (RS) BO 30 (30, 30, 32, 32) sts for back neck, knit to end—10 (12, 13, 13, 15) sts.

NEXT ROW: (WS) BO 3 (3, 4, 4, 5) sts, purl to last 2 sts, ssp (see Techniques) at neck edge—6 (8, 8, 8, 9) sts.

NEXT ROW: Ssk, knit to end—5 (7, 7, 7, 8) sts.

NEXT ROW: BO 3 (3, 4, 4, 4) sts, purl to end—2 (4, 3, 3, 4) sts.

BO all sts with RS facing.

# right front

With smaller needles, CO 35 (39, 39, 43, 47) sts.

NEXT ROW: (WS) Work Row 1 of k2, p2 rib over 34 (38, 38, 42, 46) sts, p1 (front edge st).

Keeping front edge st in St st, cont in rib patt until piece measures 2" (5 cm), ending with a WS row. Change to larger cir needle and St st.

NEXT ROW: (RS) K4 (1, 4, 6, 8), [k2tog, k3 (3, 4, 3, 8)] 5 (7, 5, 6, 3) times, k2tog, k4 (1, 3, 5, 7)—29 (31, 33, 36, 43) sts.

NEXT ROW: (WS) Purl—piece measures about 2½" (6.5 cm) from CO.

## Shape Waist and Establish Lace Pattern

NEXT ROW: (RS) Work Setup Row 1 of Foliage Lace chart over 24 sts, k2 (4, 6, 9, 16), k2tog, k1—28 (30, 32, 35, 42) sts.

note: *As you work the following instructions, work the chart pattern until Row 12 has been completed, then repeat Rows 1–12 for the Foliage Lace pattern; do not repeat the setup rows.*

Working sts outside chart patt in St st, work 11 (11, 13, 13, 13) rows even in patt.

NEXT ROW: (RS) Work 24 sts Foliage Lace chart, knit to last 3 sts, k2tog, k1—1 st dec'd.

Cont in established patts, rep the shaping of the last 12 (12, 14, 14, 14) rows 1 more time—26 (28,

30, 33, 40) sts; piece measures about 7½ (7½, 8¼, 8¼, 8¼)" (19 [19, 21, 21, 21] cm) from CO. Work even for 5 rows, ending with a WS row.

INC ROW: (RS) Work in patt to last st, M1, k1—1 st inc'd.

Cont in patt, rep the inc row every 8 rows 3 more times, working new sts in St st—30 (32, 34, 37, 44) sts. Work even until piece measures 15 (15, 15½, 15½, 16)" (38 [38, 39.5, 39.5, 40.5] cm) from CO, ending with a RS row.

## Shape Armhole

BO 4 (4, 4, 5, 7) sts at the beginning of the next WS row—26 (28, 30, 32, 37) sts. Dec 1 st at armhole edge (end of RS rows, beg of WS rows) every row 3 (3, 4, 5, 6) times—23 (25, 26, 27, 31) sts.

note: *For the smallest size, this is 1 stitch less than the full 24-stitch Foliage Lace chart; work the remaining 23 chart stitches as established.*

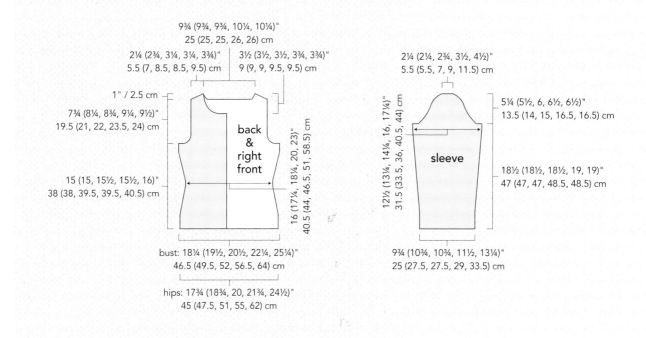

9¾ (9¾, 9¾, 10¼, 10¼)"
25 (25, 25, 26, 26) cm

2¼ (2¾, 3¼, 3¼, 3¾)"      3½ (3½, 3½, 3¾, 3¾)"
5.5 (7, 8.5, 8.5, 9.5) cm      9 (9, 9, 9.5, 9.5) cm

2¼ (2¼, 2¾, 3½, 4½)"
5.5 (5.5, 7, 9, 11.5) cm

1" / 2.5 cm

7¾ (8¼, 8¾, 9¼, 9½)"
19.5 (21, 22, 23.5, 24) cm

**back & right front**

5¼ (5½, 6, 6½, 6½)"
13.5 (14, 15, 16.5, 16.5) cm

**sleeve**

16 (17¼, 18¼, 20, 23)"
40.5 (44, 46.5, 51, 58.5) cm

12½ (13¼, 14¼, 16, 17¼)"
31.5 (33.5, 36, 40.5, 44) cm

18½ (18½, 18½, 19, 19)"
47 (47, 47, 48.5, 48.5) cm

15 (15, 15½, 15½, 16)"
38 (38, 39.5, 39.5, 40.5) cm

bust: 18¼ (19½, 20½, 22¼, 25¼)"
46.5 (49.5, 52, 56.5, 64) cm

9¾ (10¾, 10¾, 11½, 13¼)"
25 (27.5, 27.5, 29, 33.5) cm

hips: 17¾ (18¾, 20, 21¾, 24½)"
45 (47.5, 51, 55, 62) cm

Work even until armhole measures 5¼ (5¾, 6¼, 6½, 6¾)" (13.5 [14.5, 16, 16.5, 17] cm), ending with a WS row.

## Shape Front Neck

**NEXT ROW:** (RS) BO 8 sts work in patt to end—15 (17, 18, 19, 23) sts.

**note:** *During the following neck shaping, if there are not enough stitches in the chart section to work a p2tog decrease with its companion yarn-over, work the stitches in stockinette instead.*

Dec 1 st at neck edge (beg of RS rows, end of WS rows) every row 7 (7, 7, 8, 10) times—8 (10, 11, 11, 13) sts. Work even until armhole measures 7¾ (8¼, 8¾, 9¼, 9½)" (19.5 [21, 22, 23.5, 24] cm), ending with a RS row.

## Shape Shoulder

BO 3 (3, 4, 4, 5) sts at the beg of next WS row, then 3 (3, 4, 4, 4) sts at beg of foll WS row, then 2 (4, 3, 3, 4) sts at beg of next WS row—no sts rem.

# left front

With smaller needles, CO 35 (39, 39, 43, 47) sts.

**NEXT ROW:** (WS) P1 (front edge st), work Row 1 of k2, p2 rib over 34 (38, 38, 42, 46) sts.

Keeping front edge st in St st, cont in rib patt until piece measures 2" (5 cm), ending with a WS row. Change to larger cir needle and St st.

**NEXT ROW:** (RS) K4 (1, 4, 6, 8), [k2tog, k3 (3, 4, 3, 8)] 5 (7, 5, 6, 3) times, k2tog, k4 (1, 3, 5, 7)—29 (31, 33, 36, 43) sts.

**NEXT ROW:** (WS) Purl—piece measures about 2½" (6.5 cm) from CO.

## Shape Waist and Establish Lace Pattern

**NEXT ROW:** (RS) K1, ssk, k2 (4, 6, 9, 16), work Setup Row 1 of Foliage Lace chart over 24 sts—28 (30, 32, 35, 42) sts.

**note:** *As for the right front, after completing Row 12 of the chart, repeat Rows 1–12 for the Foliage Lace pattern; do not repeat the setup rows.*

Working sts outside chart patt in St st, work 11 (11, 13, 13, 13) rows even in patt.

NEXT ROW: (RS) K1, ssk, work to last 24 sts, work 24 sts Foliage Lace chart—1 st dec'd.

Cont in established patts, rep the shaping of the last 12 (12, 14, 14, 14) rows 1 more time—26 (28, 30, 33, 40) sts; piece measures about 7½ (7½, 8¼, 8¼, 8¼)" (19 [19, 21, 21, 21] cm) from CO. Work even for 5 rows, ending with a WS row.

INC ROW: (RS) K1, M1, work in patt to end—1 st inc'd.

Cont in patt, rep the inc row every 8 rows 3 more times, working new sts in St st—30 (32, 34, 37, 44) sts. Work even until piece measures 15 (15, 15½, 15½, 16)" (38 [38, 39.5, 39.5, 40.5] cm) from CO, ending with a WS row.

## Shape Armhole

BO 4 (4, 4, 5, 7) sts at the beginning of the next RS row—26 (28, 30, 32, 37) sts. Dec 1 st at armhole edge (beg of RS rows, end of WS rows) every row 3 (3, 4, 5, 6) times—23 (25, 26, 27, 31) sts.

note: *For the smallest size, work the remaining 23 Foliage Lace chart stitches as established.*

Work even until armhole measures 5¼ (5¾, 6¼, 6½, 6¾)" (13.5 [14.5, 16, 16.5, 17] cm), ending with a RS row.

## Shape Front Neck

NEXT ROW: (WS) BO 8 sts, work in patt to end—15 (17, 18, 19, 23) sts.

note: *As for the right front, if there are not enough stitches to work each decrease with its companion yarnover, work the stitches in stockinette instead.*

Dec 1 st at neck edge (end of RS rows, beg of WS rows) every row 7 (7, 7, 8, 10) times—8 (10, 11, 11, 13) sts. Work even until armhole measures 7¾ (8¼, 8¾, 9¼, 9½)" (19.5 [21, 22, 23.5, 24] cm), ending with a WS row.

## Shape Shoulder

BO 3 (3, 4, 4, 5) sts at the beg of next RS row, then 3 (3, 4, 4, 4) sts at beg of foll RS row, then 2 (4, 3, 3, 4) sts at beg of next RS row—no sts rem.

## sleeves

With smaller needles, CO 42 (46, 46, 50, 54) sts. Work in k2, p2 rib for 2½" (6.5 cm), beg and ending with a WS row. Change to larger cir needle and St st.

NEXT ROW: (RS) K2 (1, 1, 1, 1), [k2tog, k3 (4, 4, 3, 5)] 7 (7, 7, 9, 7) times, k2tog, k3 (1, 1, 2, 2)—34 (38, 38, 40, 46) sts.

## Foliage Lace

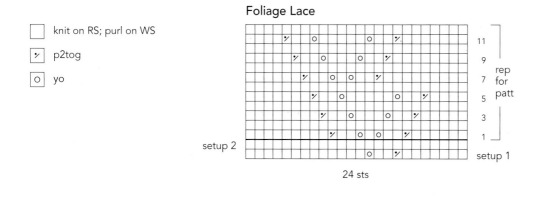

knit on RS; purl on WS

p2tog

yo

setup 2

setup 1

rep for patt

24 sts

**NEXT ROW:** (WS) Purl—piece measures about 3" (7.5 cm) from CO.

**INC ROW:** (RS) K1, M1, knit to last st, M1, k1—2 sts inc'd.

Cont in St st, rep the inc row every 18 (24, 14, 10, 12) rows 4 (3, 5, 7, 6) more times, working new sts in St st—44 (46, 50, 56, 60) sts. Work even until piece measures 18½ (18½, 18½, 19, 19)" (47 [47, 47, 48.5, 48.5] cm) from CO, ending with a WS row.

## Shape Sleeve Cap

BO 4 (4, 4, 5, 7) sts at the beginning of the next 2 rows—36 (38, 42, 46, 46) sts. Dec 1 st at each side every 4 rows 2 (2, 3, 3, 4) times, then every RS row 5 (6, 4, 7, 5) times, then every row 4 (4, 6, 6, 4) times—14 (14, 16, 18, 22) sts rem. BO 3 sts at beg of next 2 rows—8 (8, 10, 12, 16) sts rem. BO all sts.

# finishing

Block pieces to measurements. With yarn threaded on a tapestry needle, sew shoulder seams. Sew sleeves into armholes. Sew sleeve and side seams.

## Collar

With smaller needles and RS facing, pick up and knit 90 (90, 90, 94, 94) sts around neck opening. Work in k2, p2 rib until piece measures 5½" (14 cm) from pick-up row, ending with a WS row. With RS facing, BO all sts using the tubular double rib BO method (see Techniques).

## Buttonband

With smaller needles and RS facing, pick up and knit 98 (102, 110, 114, 122) sts along left front edge. Work in k2, p2 rib for 7 rows. With RS facing, BO all sts in patt.

## Buttonhole Band

With smaller needles and RS facing, pick up and knit 98 (102, 110, 114, 122) sts along right front edge. Work k2, p2 rib for 3 rows, beg and ending with a WS row.

**BUTTONHOLE ROW:** (RS) Work 6 (5, 6, 5, 6) sts in patt, [work a 3-st one-row buttonhole (see Techniques), work until there are 11 (12, 13, 14, 15) sts on right needle after buttonhole] 6 times, work a 3-st one-row buttonhole, work in patt to end—7 buttonholes completed.

Work in rib patt for 3 more rows, ending with a WS row. With RS facing, BO all sts in patt.

Weave in all loose ends. Using sewing needle and thread, sew five buttons to the RS of the left front buttonband, opposite buttonholes. Sew the rem two buttons to the WS of the left front buttonband, opposite buttonholes, so the buttons will show on the RS when the collar is folded back as shown.

# washington square

## HAT

**FINISHED SIZE**

17¼ (18, 19¾)" (44 [45.5, 50] cm) head circumference. Hat shown measures 18" (45.5 cm).

**YARN**

Chunky Weight (#5 Bulky).

**SHOWN HERE:** Cascade Yarns *Ecological Wool* (100% wool; 478 yd [437 m]/250 g): #8085 mocha, 1 skein.

**NEEDLES**

**HAT**—size U.S. 10 (6 mm): 16" (40 cm) circular (cir) needle and double-pointed needles (dpn).

**RIBBING**—size 9 (5.5 mm): 16" (40 cm) cir needle.

*Adjust needle sizes, if necessary, to obtain the correct gauge.*

**NOTIONS**

Markers (m); tapestry needle; one 1" (2.5 cm) button; sewing needle and matching thread.

**GAUGE**

14 sts and 20 rnds = 4" (10 cm) in St st on larger needles.

Keep your ears warm while you play guitar in Washington Square (as Woody Guthrie did back in the 1940s!). This hat was designed as a companion piece to the Washington Square Cardigan (see page 74). Because the yardage for the Ecological Wool yarn is so generous, there should be enough left over from the cardigan to knit the hat as well. If the cardigan doesn't interest you, one skein of this yarn will make four to five hats for your friends, depending on size.

## stitch guide

### K2, P2 RIB
**(multiple of 4 sts + 2)**

**ROW 1:** (RS) K2, *p2, k2; rep from *.

**ROW 2:** (WS) P2, *k2, p2; rep from *.

Rep Rows 1 and 2 for patt.

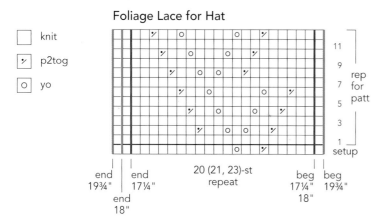

| | knit |
| | p2tog |
| | yo |

#### Foliage Lace for Hat

end 19¾"
end 17¼"
end 18"
20 (21, 23)-st repeat
beg 17¼"
18"
beg 19¾"

11
9
7 — rep for patt
5
3
1
setup

## hat

With smaller cir needle, CO 78 (82, 90) sts, do not join. Work 6 rows in k2, p2 rib (see Stitch Guide), ending with a WS row. BO 8 sts at beg of next RS row for button tab, work to end—70 (74, 82) sts rem—piece measures 1¼" (3.2 cm). Change to larger cir needle. Place marker (pm) and join for working in rnds with RS facing out.

**NEXT RND:** K10 (8, 4), [k2tog, k4] 10 (11, 13) times—60 (63, 69) sts.

**NEXT RND:** Beg and ending where indicated for your size, *work setup rnd of Foliage Lace over 20 (21, 23) sts, pm; rep from * 2 more times.

Slipping markers as you come to them (sl m), cont in patt from chart until Rnd 12 has been completed, then rep Rnds 1–12 (do not rep the setup rnd) until hat measures about 6" (15 cm) from CO, ending with Rnd 7 of chart.

### Shape Crown

**note:** *When shaping the crown, maintain the established pattern as well as possible. If there are not enough stitches to work a p2tog decrease with its companion yarnover, work the stitches in stockinette.*

**DEC RND:** *Work in patt to 2 sts before m, k2tog, sl m; rep from * 2 more times—3 sts dec'd.

Cont in patt, rep the dec rnd every other rnd 5 (5, 6) more times, changing to dpn when necessary—42 (45, 48) sts rem; 14 (15, 16) sts in each marked section.

**NEXT RND:** Removing m as you come to them, k0 (1, 0), *k2tog; rep from * to end—21 (23, 24) sts.

Cut yarn, leaving a 12" (30.5 cm) tail. Thread tail onto a tapestry needle, run needle through sts, drawstring-fashion, and pull snug to close top of hat.

## finishing

Weave in all ends. Block if desired.

Overlap button tab on top of ribbed band and use sewing needle and thread to sew button through both layers of knitting, centered on tab as shown.

# union square
## COWL

**FINISHED SIZE**
About 9½" (24 cm) wide and 60"
(152.5 cm) long.

**YARN**
Worsted Weight (#4 Medium).

**SHOWN HERE:** Malabrigo *Merino*
*Worsted* (100% merino wool; 210 yd
[192 m]/100 g): #63 natural, 3 skeins.

**NEEDLES**
Size U.S. 9 (5.5 mm): straight.

*Adjust needle size, if necessary, to*
*obtain the correct gauge.*

**NOTIONS**
Markers (m); cable needle (cn); tapestry
needle; five ⅞" (22 mm) buttons, sewing
needle and matching thread.

**GAUGE**
21½ sts and 23 rows = 4" (10 cm) in patt
from Cable and Ladder chart.

Wend your way through the farmer's market without catching a chill and sip a steaming cup of hot cider while staring up at the statue of Abraham Lincoln. This is a perfect project for a beginner looking to jump into something a little more challenging. The cable pattern is repeated across the row with a simple textured seed-stitch border. Since the ends are buttoned together, it can be worn in several different ways—try it unbuttoned as a scarf or wrapped once or twice around the neck and shoulders for a cowl.

## stitch guide

### SEED STITCH
### (worked over an odd number of sts)

ALL ROWS: P1, *k1, p1; rep from *.

Rep this row for patt.

## notes

⊖ This piece is fairly long for a cowl and can be wrapped once or twice around the neck. Feel free to shorten it a bit if the length doesn't suit you. As you are knitting, just wrap the piece around your neck to check the fit and drape, and when it seems right to you, just skip to the seed stitch top border section, work the buttonholes, and you're all set!

⊖ The stitch to the left of a cable crossing can sometimes be pulled out of shape very easily. To help minimize this, give the yarn an extra tug after knitting the last stitch of the cable and again after working the following stitch.

## cowl

CO 51 sts. Work in seed st patt (see Stitch Guide) for 6 rows. Work WS setup row of Cable and Ladder chart once, then rep Rows 1–8 of chart (do not rep the setup row) until piece measures about 59" (150 cm) from CO, or 1" (2.5 cm) less than desired length, ending with Row 2 or Row 6 of chart so the first and last cables of the piece will each be 1 row away from the seed st border. Work all sts in seed st for 2 rows.

BUTTONHOLE ROW: (RS) Work 3 seed sts, [yo, k2tog, work 9 seed sts] 4 times, yo, k2tog, work 2 seed sts—5 buttonholes completed.

Work 2 rows in established seed st. BO all sts in seed st patt.

## finishing

Block to measurements. Weave in all loose ends. Sew buttons to RS of seed st border at beg of cowl, opposite buttonholes in border at end of cowl.

| | knit on RS; purl on WS |
|---|---|
| • | purl on RS; knit on WS |
| ╱ | p2tog on WS |
| ╲ | ssk on RS |
| o | yo on RS and WS |
| | pattern repeat |

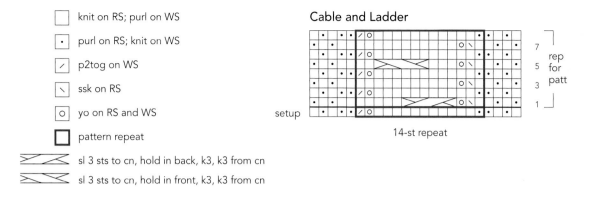

sl 3 sts to cn, hold in back, k3, k3 from cn

sl 3 sts to cn, hold in front, k3, k3 from cn

## Cable and Ladder

setup

14-st repeat

7
5
3
1

rep for patt

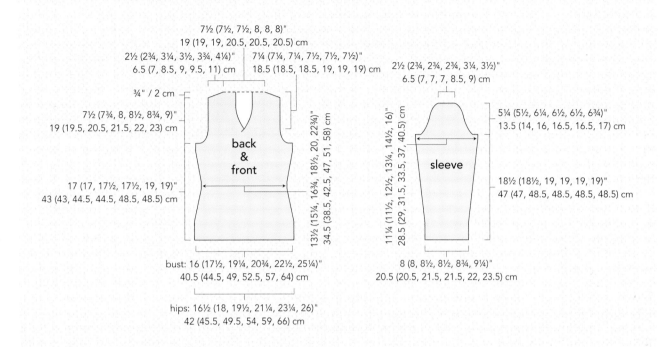

**7½ (7½, 7½, 8, 8, 8)"**
19 (19, 19, 20.5, 20.5, 20.5) cm

**2½ (2¾, 3¼, 3½, 3¾, 4¼)"**
6.5 (7, 8.5, 9, 9.5, 11) cm

**7¼ (7¼, 7¼, 7½, 7½, 7½)"**
18.5 (18.5, 18.5, 19, 19, 19) cm

**2½ (2¾, 2¾, 2¾, 3¼, 3½)"**
6.5 (7, 7, 7, 8.5, 9) cm

**¾" / 2 cm**

**7½ (7¾, 8, 8½, 8¾, 9)"**
19 (19.5, 20.5, 21.5, 22, 23) cm

**5¼ (5½, 6¼, 6½, 6½, 6¾)"**
13.5 (14, 16, 16.5, 16.5, 17) cm

back & front

sleeve

**13½ (15¼, 16¾, 18½, 20, 22¾)"**
34.5 (38.5, 42.5, 47, 51, 58) cm

**11¼ (11½, 12½, 13¼, 14½, 16)"**
28.5 (29, 31.5, 33.5, 37, 40.5) cm

**17 (17, 17½, 17½, 19, 19)"**
43 (43, 44.5, 44.5, 48.5, 48.5) cm

**18½ (18½, 19, 19, 19, 19)"**
47 (47, 48.5, 48.5, 48.5, 48.5) cm

**bust: 16 (17½, 19¼, 20¾, 22½, 25¼)"**
40.5 (44.5, 49, 52.5, 57, 64) cm

**8 (8, 8½, 8½, 8¾, 9¼)"**
20.5 (20.5, 21.5, 21.5, 22, 23.5) cm

**hips: 16½ (18, 19½, 21¼, 23¼, 26)"**
42 (45.5, 49.5, 54, 59, 66) cm

74, 78, 82) sts rem. Cont in patt until armholes measure 7½ (7¾, 8, 8½, 8¾, 9)" (19 [19.5, 20.5, 21.5, 22, 23] cm), ending with a WS row. Make a note of the stripe patt row just completed so you can end the front armholes with the same row to match.

## Shape Shoulders

BO 4 (5, 5, 5, 6, 7) sts at beg of next 4 rows, then BO 5 (4, 6, 7, 7, 7) sts at beg of foll 2 rows—38 (38, 38, 40, 40, 40) back neck sts rem. Place sts on holder. Make a note of the last WS stripe patt row completed so you can begin the hood with the correct row later.

# front

Work as for back until armhole shaping has been completed—64 (66, 70, 74, 78, 82) sts rem. Work even until armholes measure 1 (1¼, 1½, 1¾, 2, 2¼)" (2.5 [3.2, 3.8, 4.5, 5, 5.5] cm), ending with a WS row.

## Shape Front Neck

**NEXT ROW:** (RS) K29 (30, 32, 34, 36, 38), k1f&b (see Techniques) 6 times, k29 (30, 32, 34, 36, 38)—6 sts inc'd at center.

**NEXT ROW:** (WS) P29 (30, 32, 34, 36, 38), [k1, sl next st to cn held in back, p1, sl next st to cn held in back] 3 times, place 6 sts on cn and rem 29 (30, 32, 34, 36, 38) unworked sts on holder—35 (36, 38, 40, 42, 44) right front sts rem on needle.

### Right front neck

Cont on sts of right front as foll:

**NEXT ROW:** (RS) [K1, p1] 3 times, knit to end.

Keeping 6 sts at neck edge (beg of RS rows, end of WS rows) in k1, p1 rib as established, work even for 3 more rows, ending with a WS row.

**DEC ROW:** (RS) [K1, p1] 3 times, ssk, knit to end—1 st dec'd.

Cont in patt, rep the dec row every 6 rows 5 more times—29 (30, 32, 34, 36, 38) sts rem. Work even until armhole measures 7½ (7¾, 8, 8½, 8¾, 9)" (19 [19.5, 20.5, 21.5, 22, 23] cm), ending with the same WS stripe patt row as the back.

### Right front shoulder

Knit 1 RS row. BO 4 (5, 5, 5, 6, 7) sts at the beginning of the next 2 WS rows, then BO 5 (4, 6, 7, 7, 7) sts at the beginning of the next WS row—16 (16, 16, 17, 17, 17) sts rem. Place sts on holder.

### Left front neck

Return 35 (36, 38, 40, 42, 44) held left front sts to needle and rejoin yarn to neck edge with WS facing.

**NEXT ROW:** (WS) [P1, k1] 3 times, purl to end.

Keeping 6 sts at neck edge (end of RS rows, beg of WS rows) in k1, p1 rib as established, work even for 4 more rows, ending with a WS row.

**DEC ROW:** (RS) Work in patt to last 8 sts, k2tog, [p1, k1] 3 times—1 st dec'd.

Cont in patt, rep the dec row every 6 rows 5 more times—29 (30, 32, 34, 36, 38) sts rem. Work even until armhole measures 7½ (7¾, 8, 8½, 8¾, 9)" (19 [19.5, 20.5, 21.5, 22, 23] cm), ending with the same WS stripe patt row as the back and right front.

### Left front shoulder

BO 4 (5, 5, 5, 6, 7) sts at the beginning of the next 2 RS rows, then BO 5 (4, 6, 7, 7, 7) sts at the beginning of the next RS row, then work 1 WS row even—16 (16, 16, 17, 17, 17) sts rem. Place sts on holder.

## sleeves

With waste yarn and crochet hook, use the crochet chain provisional method to CO 40 (40, 42, 42, 44, 46) sts onto straight needle. Change to A, work 5 rows in St st, beg and ending with a WS row. Purl 1 RS row for hem fold line. Work 5 more rows in St st, ending with a WS row. Carefully undo provisional CO and place sts from base of CO on second straight needle. With RS facing, fold hem along fold line to bring needles

together and parallel, with needle holding provisional CO sts in back.

**NEXT ROW:** (RS) Using cir needle, *insert needle tip into the first st on the front needle, then into the first st on the back needle and work these 2 sts tog as k2tog; rep from * to end—40 (40, 42, 42, 44, 46) sts on one needle; finished hem measures about ¾" (2 cm) from fold line.

Change to Stripe Pattern II (II, II, II, I, I) (see Stitch Guide), and work until piece measures 3" (7.5 cm) from fold line, ending with a WS row.

**INC ROW:** (RS) K1, M1, knit to last st, M1, k1— 2 sts inc'd.

Cont in patt rep the inc row every 0 (12, 10, 8, 0, 6) rows 0 (5, 2, 3, 0, 12) more times, then every 14 (14, 12, 10, 8, 8) rows 7 (3, 7, 8, 13, 4) times, working new sts in St st—56 (58, 62, 66, 72, 80) sts. Work even until piece measures about 18½ (18½, 19, 19, 19, 19)" (47 [47, 48.5, 48.5, 48.5, 48.5] cm) from fold line, ending with the same WS stripe patt row as the lower body of the back and front.

## Shape Sleeve Cap

BO 5 (6, 7, 8, 9, 10) sts at beg of next 2 rows—46 (46, 48, 50, 54, 60) sts. Dec 1 st at each side every RS row 2 (0, 2, 0, 0, 0) times, then every 4 rows 5 (7, 7, 8, 8, 8) times, then every RS row 2 (1, 2, 3, 2, 2) time(s), then every row 5 (5, 3, 4, 6, 8) times—18 (20, 20, 20, 22, 24) sts rem. BO 3 sts at beg of next 2 rows—12 (14, 14, 14, 16, 18) sts rem. BO all sts.

# finishing

Block pieces to measurements. With yarn threaded on a tapestry needle, sew shoulder seams. Sew sleeves into armholes. Sew sleeve and side seams.

## Hood

With RS facing, place 16 (16, 16, 17, 17, 17) held right front sts on cir needle, place first 19 (19, 19, 20, 20, 20) held back neck sts on needle, place marker (pm) at center back, place last 19 (19, 19, 20, 20, 20) back neck sts on needle, place 16 (16, 16, 17, 17, 17) left front sts on needle—70 (70, 70, 74, 74, 74) sts. Rejoin yarn with RS facing at right neck edge. Keeping 6 sts at each end of row in k1, p1 rib as established, resume working in stripe patt and work even for 1" (2.5 cm), ending with a WS row.

INC ROW: (RS) Work 6 rib sts, k1, M1, work to 1 st before center back m, M1, k1, slip marker (sl m), k1, M1, work to last 7 sts, M1, k1, work 6 rib sts—4 sts inc'd.

Cont in patt and working new sts in St st, rep the inc row every 4 rows 2 (2, 2, 3, 3, 3) more times, then every 6 rows 2 times, working new sts in St st—90 (90, 90, 98, 98, 98) sts. Work 5 rows even, beg and ending with a WS row.

CENTER BACK INC ROW: Work to 1 st before center back m, M1, k1, sl m, k1, M1, work to end—2 sts inc'd.

Cont in patt and working new sts in St st, rep the center back inc row every 4 rows 4 more times—100 (100, 100, 108, 108, 108) sts; hood measures about 7¼ (7¼, 7¼, 7¾, 7¾, 7¾)" (18.5 [18.5, 18.5, 19.5, 19.5, 19.5] cm). Work even until hood measures 10 (10, 10, 10½, 10½, 10½)" (25.5 [25.5, 25.5, 26.5, 26.5, 26.5] cm), ending with a WS row.

NEXT ROW: (RS) Work to 2 sts before center back m, k2tog, remove m, place rem 50 (50, 50, 54, 54, 54) sts on holder—49 (49, 49, 53, 53, 53) right hood sts rem on needle.

## Right hood

NEXT ROW: (WS) Work even.

NEXT ROW: (RS) Work to last 2 sts, k2tog—1 st dec'd.

Cont in patt, rep the shaping of the last 2 rows 5 (5, 5, 7, 7, 7) more times—43 (43, 43, 45, 45, 45) sts rem.

NEXT ROW: (WS) P2tog, work to end—1 st dec'd.

NEXT ROW: (RS) Work to last 2 sts, k2tog—1 st dec'd.

Rep the last 2 rows 0 (0, 0, 1, 1, 1) time(s), then work the WS dec row once more—40 sts rem for all sizes. Work 1 RS row even. BO 5 sts at beg of next 4 WS rows, ending with the final BO row—20 sts rem; hood measures about 13½ (13½, 13½, 14¾, 14¾, 14¾)" (34.5 [34.5, 34.5, 37.5, 37.5, 37.5] cm). BO all sts.

## Left hood

Return 50 (50, 50, 54, 54, 54) held left hood sts to needle and rejoin yarn with RS facing.

NEXT ROW: (RS) Ssk, work to end—1 st dec'd.

NEXT ROW: (WS) Work even.

Cont in patt, rep the shaping of the last 2 rows 5 (5, 5, 7, 7, 7) more times—43 (43, 43, 45, 45, 45) sts rem.

NEXT ROW: (RS) Ssk, work to end—1 st dec'd.

NEXT ROW: (WS) Work to last 2 sts, ssp (see Techniques)—1 st dec'd.

Rep the last 2 rows 0 (0, 0, 1, 1, 1) time(s), then work the RS dec row once more—40 sts rem for all sizes. Work 1 WS row even. BO 5 sts at beg of next 4 RS rows, the work 1 WS row even—20 sts rem; hood measures about 13½ (13½, 13½, 14¾, 14¾, 14¾)" (34.5 [34.5, 34.5, 37.5, 37.5, 37.5] cm). BO all sts.

Sew seam at top of hood. Weave in all loose ends.

# atrium CARDIGAN

## FINISHED SIZE

32½ (35¼, 37¾, 40, 45, 49)" (82.5 [89.5, 96, 101.5, 114.5, 124.5] cm) bust circumference, buttoned, including 1" (2.5 cm) front band. Cardigan shown measures 35¼" (89.5 cm).

## YARN

Sportweight (#2 Fine).

**SHOWN HERE:** Manos del Uruguay *Serena* (60% baby alpaca, 40% pima cotton; 170 yd [155 m]/50 g): #2144 flamingo, 4 (4, 5, 5, 6, 6) skeins.

## NEEDLES

**BODY AND SLEEVES**—size U.S. 6 (4 mm): 24" (61 cm) circular (cir) needle.

**RIBBING**—size 3 (3.25 mm) 24" (61 cm) cir needle.

*Adjust needle sizes, if necessary, to obtain the correct gauge.*

## NOTIONS

Markers (m); stitch holders; tapestry needle; six ⅝" (16 mm) buttons; sewing needle and thread to match buttons.

## GAUGE

18 sts and 28 rows = 4" (10 cm) in Roman Stripe patt (see Notes) on larger needles.

If there was one piece in this book that screamed "Spring!" this cardigan would be it. The open stitch worked in a cheery pink color says it all. With a little bit of a vintage feeling, this is the type of cardigan that I could easily knit in a few different colors to match all my new spring purchases. If you are looking for an easy-to-wear cardigan that will never go out of style, this would be my pick: It is understated, yet stands out, like a serene spot in a bustling plaza.

## stitch guide

### K1, P1 RIB
*(worked over an odd number of sts)*

ROW 1: (RS) K1, *p1, k1; rep from *.

ROW 2: (WS) P1, *k1, p1; rep from *.

Rep Rows 1 and 2 for patt.

### K1, P1 RIB
*(worked over an even number of sts)*

ALL ROWS: *K1, p1; rep from *.

Rep this row for patt.

### ROMAN STRIPE
*(worked on an even number of patt sts + 4 edge sts)*

ROW 1: K2 (edge sts, knit every row), *yo, k1; rep from * to last 2 sts, k2 (edge sts, knit every row)—sts have inc'd to twice the original patt sts, plus 2 edge sts at each side.

ROW 2: K2, purl to last 2 sts, k2.

ROW 3: K2, *k2tog; rep from * to last 2 sts, k2—sts have dec'd to original number.

ROWS 4 AND 5: K2, *yo, k2tog; rep from to last 2 sts, k2.

ROWS 6 AND 7: Knit.

Rep Rows 1–7 for patt; see Notes.

## notes

⊖ The lower body is worked in one piece to the armholes, then the fronts and back are divided for working separately to the shoulders.

⊖ The stitch count of the Roman Stripe pattern does not remain constant throughout. It temporarily increases for Rows 1 and 2, then decreases back to the original stitch count in Row 3. Always count stitches for the gauge swatch and during shaping after completing Rows 3, 4, 5, 6, or 7 of the pattern when the original stitch count has been restored.

⊖ The Roman Stripe pattern repeats over an odd number of rows, which means that the fabric does not have defined right and wrong sides. For example, if you work a repeat with Rows 1, 3, 5, and 7 as RS rows, the following repeat will begin with Row 1 as a WS row, and Rows 3, 5, and 7 will be WS rows for the rest of this repeat. Because both sides of the fabric appear similar, you may find it helpful for shaping purposes to mark the RS of each piece with a removable marker or scrap yarn.

## body

With smaller cir needle, CO 177 (189, 207, 219, 245, 269) sts. Do not join. Work k1, p1 rib (see Stitch Guide) until piece measures 2" (5 cm), ending with a WS row. Change to larger needles.

NEXT ROW: (RS) K2 (9, 2, 3, 6, 3), [k2tog, k3] 34 (34, 40, 42, 46, 52) times, k2tog, k3 (8, 3, 4, 7, 4)—142 (154, 166, 176, 198, 216) sts.

NEXT ROW: (WS) Knit.

Change to Roman Stripe patt (see Stitch Guide) beg with a RS row, and work even in patt until piece measures 12 (12¼, 12¾, 13¼, 14, 14¼)" (30.5 [31, 32.5, 33.5, 35.5, 36] cm) from CO, ending with WS Row 4 or 6 of patt (see Notes).

### Shape Front Neck

NECK DEC ROW: (RS) Ssk (see Techniques), work in patt to last 2 sts, k2tog—2 sts dec'd.

Cont in patt, rep the neck dec row every 4 (2, 2, 2, 4, 4) rows 3 (4, 1, 1, 1, 1) time(s), then every 0 (4, 4, 4, 0, 0) rows 0 (1, 2, 1, 0, 0) time(s), then work 1 WS row even—134 (142, 158, 170, 194, 212) sts rem (see Notes); piece measures about 14 (14¼, 14½, 14½, 14¾, 15)" (35.5 [36, 37, 37, 37.5, 38] cm) from CO.

### Divide Fronts and Back

NEXT ROW: (RS) Work 25 (27, 32, 34, 39, 42) right front sts in patt, BO 10 (10, 10, 12, 14, 18) sts, work in patt until there are 64 (68, 74, 78, 88, 92) sts on right needle after BO gap, BO 10 (10, 10, 12, 14, 18) sts, work 25 (27, 32, 34, 39, 42) left front sts.

Place right front and back sts on separate holders—25 (27, 32, 34, 39, 42) left front sts rem on needle.

## left front

**note:** *Neck shaping continues while armhole shaping is introduced; read the next sections all the way through before proceeding.*

For armhole shaping, work 1 WS row even, then dec 1 st at armhole edge (beg of RS rows, end of WS rows) every row 3 (3, 3, 3, 5, 5) times, then every RS row 1 (2, 3, 3, 4, 4) time(s)—4 (5, 6, 6, 9, 9) sts total removed at armhole edge.

*At the same time,* resume established neck shaping by dec 1 st at neck edge (end of RS rows) on the 4th row after the previous dec row, then every 4 rows 10 (10, 12, 13, 13, 14) more times—11 (11, 13, 14, 14, 15) more sts removed at neck edge.

When all armhole and neck shaping has been completed—10 (11, 13, 14, 16, 18) sts rem. Work even until armhole measures 7¼ (7½, 7¾, 8¼, 8¾, 9)" (18.5 [19, 19.5, 21, 22, 23] cm), ending with a WS row.

### Shape Shoulder

BO 3 (4, 4, 5, 5, 6) sts at beg of next 2 RS rows, then BO 4 (3, 5, 4, 6, 6) sts at beg of next RS row—no sts rem.

### Right Front

**note:** *As for left front, armhole and neck shaping are worked at the same time; read the next sections all the way through before proceeding.*

Return 25 (27, 32, 34, 39, 42) right front sts to larger cir needle and rejoin yarn with WS facing.

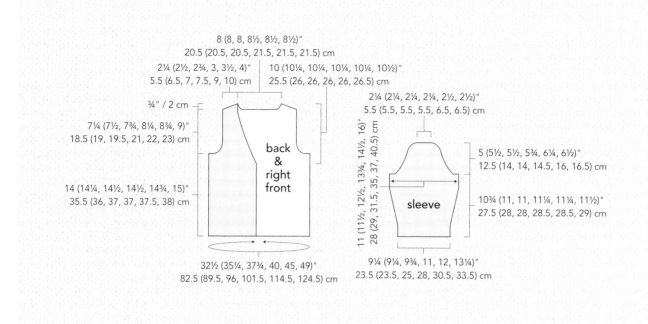

8 (8, 8, 8½, 8½, 8½)"
20.5 (20.5, 20.5, 21.5, 21.5, 21.5) cm

2¼ (2½, 2¾, 3, 3½, 4)"
5.5 (6.5, 7, 7.5, 9, 10) cm

10 (10¼, 10¼, 10¼, 10¼, 10½)"
25.5 (26, 26, 26, 26, 26.5) cm

¾" / 2 cm

7¼ (7½, 7¾, 8¼, 8¾, 9)"
18.5 (19, 19.5, 21, 22, 23) cm

14 (14¼, 14½, 14½, 14¾, 15)"
35.5 (36, 37, 37, 37.5, 38) cm

back & right front

32½ (35¼, 37¾, 40, 45, 49)"
82.5 (89.5, 96, 101.5, 114.5, 124.5) cm

2¼ (2¼, 2¼, 2¼, 2½, 2½)"
5.5 (5.5, 5.5, 5.5, 6.5, 6.5) cm

11 (11½, 12½, 13¾, 14½, 16)"
28 (29, 31.5, 35, 37, 40.5) cm

sleeve

5 (5½, 5½, 5¾, 6¼, 6½)"
12.5 (14, 14, 14.5, 16, 16.5) cm

10¾ (11, 11, 11¼, 11¼, 11½)"
27.5 (28, 28, 28.5, 28.5, 29) cm

9¼ (9¼, 9¾, 11, 12, 13¼)"
23.5 (23.5, 25, 28, 30.5, 33.5) cm

For armhole shaping, work 1 WS row even, then dec 1 st at armhole edge (end of RS rows, beg of WS rows) every row 3 (3, 3, 3, 5, 5) times, then every RS row 1 (2, 3, 3, 4, 4) time(s)—4 (5, 6, 6, 9, 9) sts total removed at armhole edge.

*At the same time*, resume established neck shaping by dec 1 st at neck edge (beg of RS rows) on the 4th row after the previous neck dec row, then every 4 rows 10 (10, 12, 13, 13, 14) more times—11 (11, 13, 14, 14, 15) more sts removed at neck edge.

When all armhole and neck shaping has been completed—10 (11, 13, 14, 16, 18) sts rem. Work even until armhole measures 7¼ (7½, 7¾, 8¼, 8¾, 9)" (18.5 [19, 19.5, 21, 22, 23] cm), ending with a RS row.

## Shape Shoulder

BO 3 (4, 4, 5, 5, 6) sts at beg of next 2 WS rows, then BO 4 (3, 5, 4, 6, 6) sts at beg of next WS row—no sts rem.

# back

Return 64 (68, 74, 78, 88, 92) held back sts to larger cir needle and rejoin yarn with WS facing. Work 1 WS row even. Dec 1 st at each side every row 3 (3, 3, 5, 5) times, then every RS row 1 (2, 3, 3, 4, 4) time(s)—56 (58, 62, 66, 70, 74) sts rem. Work even until armholes measure 7¼ (7½, 7¾, 8¼, 8¾, 9)" (18.5 [19, 19.5, 21, 22, 23] cm), ending with a WS row.

## Shape Back Neck and Shoulders

NEXT ROW: (RS) BO 3 (4, 4, 5, 5, 6) sts, work in patt until there are 9 (9, 11, 11, 13, 14) sts on right needle after BO, place rem 44 (45, 47, 50, 52, 54) sts on holder—9 (9, 11, 11, 13, 14) right back shoulder sts rem on needle.

### Right shoulder

NEXT ROW: (WS) P2tog at neck edge, work to end—8 (8, 10, 10, 12, 13) sts.

NEXT ROW: (RS) BO 3 (4, 4, 5, 5, 6) sts, work to last 2 sts, k2tog—4 (3, 5, 4, 6, 6) sts.

**NEXT ROW:** Work even.

BO rem sts.

### Left shoulder

Return 44 (45, 47, 50, 52, 54) held sts to larger cir needle with RS facing and rejoin yarn.

**NEXT ROW:** (RS) BO 32 (32, 32, 34, 34, 34) back neck sts, work to end—12 (13, 15, 16, 18, 20) sts.

**NEXT ROW:** (WS) BO 3 (4, 4, 5, 5, 6) sts, work to last 2 sts, ssp (see Techniques) at neck edge—8 (8, 10, 10, 12, 13) sts.

**NEXT ROW:** Ssk, work to end—7 (7, 9, 9, 11, 12) sts.

**NEXT ROW:** BO 3 (4, 4, 5, 5, 6) sts, work to end—4 (3, 5, 4, 6, 6) sts.

**NEXT ROW:** Work even.

BO rem sts.

## sleeves

With smaller cir needle, CO 54 (54, 56, 60, 64, 68) sts. Do not join. Work k1, p1 rib until piece measures 1¾" (4.5 cm), ending with a WS row. Change to larger cir needle.

**NEXT ROW:** (RS) K4 (4, 5, 2, 4, 5), [k2tog, k2 (2, 2, 4, 4, 6)] 11 (11, 11, 9, 9, 7) times, k2tog, k4 (4, 5, 2, 4, 5)—42 (42, 44, 50, 54, 60) sts.

Change to Roman Stripe patt beg with a WS row and work 1 WS row even.

**INC ROW:** (RS) K1, M1 (see Techniques), work in patt to last st, M1, k1—2 sts inc'd.

Cont in patt, rep the inc row every 14 (10, 8, 10, 10, 10) rows 2 (1, 2, 5, 5, 4) more time(s), then every 16 (12, 10, 0, 0, 12) rows 1 (3, 3, 0, 0, 1) time(s), working new sts into patt—50 (52, 56, 62, 66, 72) sts.

Work even in patt until piece measures 10¾ (11, 11, 11¼, 11¼, 11½)" (27.5 [28, 28, 28.5, 28.5, 29] cm) from CO, ending with WS Row 4 or 6 of patt.

### Shape Sleeve Cap

BO 5 (5, 5, 6, 7, 9) sts at beg of next 2 rows—40 (42, 46, 50, 52, 54) sts. Dec 1 st each end of needle every 4 rows 5 (6, 5, 4, 5, 6) times, then every RS row 4 (4, 5, 7, 8, 6) times, then every row 3 (3, 5, 6, 4, 6) times—16 (16, 16, 16, 18, 18) sts rem. BO 3 sts at the beginning of the next 2 rows—10 (10, 10, 10, 12, 12) sts. BO all sts.

# finishing

Block pieces to measurements. With yarn threaded on a tapestry needle, sew shoulder seams. Sew sleeves into armholes.

### Front Band

With smaller cir needle and RS facing, beg at lower right front corner pick up and knit 67 (68, 71, 73, 78, 79) sts along right front to start of neck shaping, 56 (57, 58, 58, 58, 58) sts to right shoulder seam, 45 (45, 45, 47, 47, 47) sts across back neck to left shoulder seam, 56 (57, 58, 58, 58, 58) sts along left front neck to start of neck shaping, and 67 (68, 71, 73, 78, 79) sts to lower left front corner—291 (295, 303, 309, 319, 321) sts. Work in k1, p1 rib for 3 rows, beg and ending with a WS row.

BUTTONHOLE ROW: (RS) Work 5 sts, [work 3-st one-row buttonhole (see Techniques), work 7 (7, 8, 8, 9, 9) sts] 5 times, work 3-st one-row buttonhole, work to end—6 buttonholes completed.

Work k1, p1 rib for 3 rows, beg and ending with a WS row. BO all sts in rib patt.

Weave in all loose ends. Using sewing needle and thread, sew buttons to left front band, opposite buttonholes.

# brooklyn bridge
## CARDIGAN

### FINISHED SIZE

32 (35, 37½, 40½, 44, 48, 52)" (81.5 [89, 95, 103, 112, 122, 132] cm) bust circumference with fronts meeting at center. Cardigan shown measures 32" (81.5 cm).

### YARN

Fingering Weight (#1 Super Fine).

**SHOWN HERE:** Lorna's Laces *Shepherd Sock* (80% superwash merino wool, 20% nylon; 430 yd [393 m]/100 g): poppy, 4 (5, 5, 5, 6, 6, 6) skeins.

### NEEDLES

**BODY AND SLEEVES**—size U.S. 4 (3.5 mm): 24" (61 cm) circular (cir).

*Adjust needle size, if necessary, to obtain the correct gauge.*

### NOTIONS

Markers (m); stitch holders; tapestry needle.

### GAUGE

27 sts and 34 rows = 4" (10 cm) in St st.

15 to 19 sts of Triple Leaf chart (see Notes) measure 2¼" (5.5 cm) wide.

3-stitch I-cord edgings measure about ¼" (6 mm) wide each.

This cardigan is an easy addition to anyone's spring wardrobe. Its open front allows you to show off a lovely dress or your favorite printed T. The fabric created by the fingering-weight wool feels light but gives you just the right amount of warmth for chilly air-conditioned rooms, a walk in the city at night, or a breezy afternoon at Brooklyn Bridge Park.

# stitch guide

## I-CORD EDGING
*(worked over 3 edge sts)*

RIGHT FRONT: On RS rows, work first 3 sts as k3; and on WS rows, work the last 3 sts as sl 3 purlwise with yarn in front (pwise wyf).

LEFT FRONT: On RS rows, work the last 3 sts as sl 3 as if to purl with yarn in back (pwise wyb); and on WS rows, work the first 3 sts as p3.

# notes

⊖ I-cord edging makes a nice clean finish along the front edges and hood of this cardigan. In this project, it is especially helpful for two reasons. First, it eliminates the extra finishing step of picking up and working front band stitches. Second, when the hood is folded back there is no visible pick-up ridge to ruin the clean look of the cardigan.

⊖ The stitch count of the Triple Leaf chart does not remain constant throughout. It begins with 15 stitches in Rows 1–4, increases to 17 stitches in Rows 5 and 6, then increases again to 19 stitches in Rows 7 and 8, then decreases back to 15 stitches again for Rows 11 and 12. Always count the stitches of each panel as 15 stitches, even if the pattern is on a row where the stitch count has temporarily increased.

# back

CO 116 (126, 134, 144, 158, 176, 190) sts. Beg with a WS row, work 8 rows in St st, ending with a RS row. Knit 1 WS row for hem fold line. Work in St st until piece measures 4" (10 cm) from fold line, ending with a WS row.

## Shape Waist

DEC ROW: (RS) K1, ssk (see Techniques), knit to last 3 sts, k2tog, k1—2 sts dec'd.

Cont in St st, rep the dec row every 6 (6, 6, 6, 6, 4, 4) rows 4 (4, 3, 3, 3, 1, 1) more time(s), then every 8 (8, 8, 8, 8, 6, 6) rows 6 (6, 7, 7, 7, 12, 12) times—94 (104, 112, 122, 136, 148, 162) sts; piece measures about 12½ (12½, 12¾, 12¾, 12¾, 13, 13)" (31.5 [31.5, 32.5, 32.5, 32.5, 33, 33] cm) from fold line. Work even for 11 rows, beg and ending with a WS row.

INC ROW: (RS) K1, M1 (see Techniques), work to last st, M1, k1—2 sts inc'd.

Cont in St st, rep the inc row every 6 (6, 6, 6, 8, 8, 8) rows 4 (4, 3, 3, 2, 6, 6) more times, then every 8 (8, 8, 8, 10, 0, 0) rows 2 (2, 3, 3, 3, 0, 0) times, working new sts in St st—108 (118, 126, 136, 148, 162, 176) sts. Work even in St st until piece measures 19½ (19½, 20, 20, 20½, 21, 21)" (49.5 [49.5, 51, 51, 52, 53.5, 53.5] cm) from fold line, ending with a WS row.

## Shape Armholes

BO 7 (7, 8, 9, 10, 12, 14) sts at beg of next 2 rows—94 (104, 110, 118, 128, 138, 148) sts. Dec 1 st at each side every row 5 (6, 7, 9, 10, 12, 15) times—84 (92, 96, 100, 108, 114, 118) sts rem. Cont in St st until armholes measure 7¾ (7¾, 8, 8¼, 8½, 8¾, 9¼)" (19.5 [19.5, 20.5, 21, 21.5, 22, 23.5] cm), ending with a WS row.

## Shape Shoulders

BO 6 (7, 8, 8, 10, 10, 11) sts at the beg of the next 4 rows, then BO 7 (8, 8, 9, 9, 10, 10) sts at the beg of the next 2 rows—46 (48, 48, 50, 50, 54, 54) center back neck sts rem. Place sts on holder.

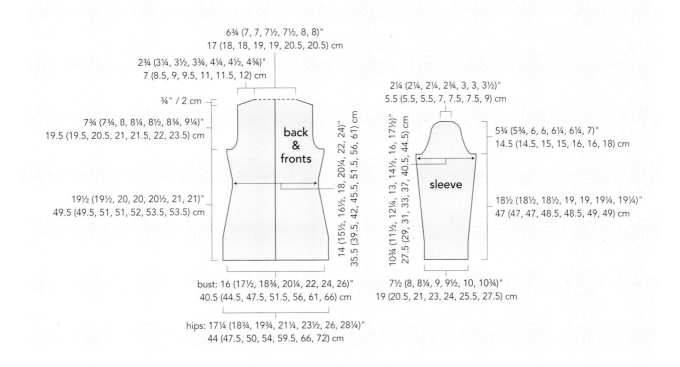

6¾ (7, 7, 7½, 7½, 8, 8)"
17 (18, 18, 19, 19, 20.5, 20.5) cm

2¾ (3¼, 3½, 3¾, 4¼, 4½, 4¾)"
7 (8.5, 9, 9.5, 11, 11.5, 12) cm

¾" / 2 cm

7¾ (7¾, 8, 8¼, 8½, 8¾, 9¼)"
19.5 (19.5, 20.5, 21, 21.5, 22, 23.5) cm

back & fronts

19½ (19½, 20, 20, 20½, 21, 21)"
49.5 (49.5, 51, 51, 52, 53.5, 53.5) cm

14 (15½, 16½, 18, 20¼, 22, 24)"
35.5 (39.5, 42, 45.5, 51.5, 56, 61) cm

bust: 16 (17½, 18¾, 20¼, 22, 24, 26)"
40.5 (44.5, 47.5, 51.5, 56, 61, 66) cm

hips: 17¼ (18¾, 19¾, 21¼, 23½, 26, 28¼)"
44 (47.5, 50, 54, 59.5, 66, 72) cm

2¼ (2¼, 2¼, 2¾, 3, 3, 3½)"
5.5 (5.5, 5.5, 7, 7.5, 7.5, 9) cm

5¾ (5¾, 6, 6, 6¼, 6¼, 7)"
14.5 (14.5, 15, 15, 16, 16, 18) cm

sleeve

10¾ (11½, 12¼, 13, 14½, 16, 17½)"
27.5 (29, 31, 33, 37, 40.5, 44.5) cm

18½ (18½, 18½, 19, 19, 19¼, 19¼)"
47 (47, 47, 48.5, 48.5, 49, 49) cm

7½ (8, 8¼, 9, 9½, 10, 10¾)"
19 (20.5, 21, 23, 24, 25.5, 27.5) cm

# right front

CO 58 (63, 67, 72, 79, 88, 95) sts. Beg with a WS row, work 8 rows in St st, ending with a RS row.

NEXT ROW: (WS) Knit to end for fold line, then use the knitted method (see Techniques) to CO 3 sts at end of row—61 (66, 70, 75, 82, 91, 98) sts.

Working 3 new CO sts at front edge in I-cord edging (see Stitch Guide), work 8 rows in St st, ending with a WS row.

NEXT ROW: (RS) Work 3 edging sts as established, k3, place marker (pm), work Row 1 of Triple Leaf chart over 15 sts, pm, knit to end.

Working patts as established, work even until piece measures 4" (10 cm) from fold line, ending with a WS row.

## Shape Waist

DEC ROW: (RS) Work in patt to last 3 sts, k2tog, k1—1 st dec'd.

Cont in patt, rep the dec row every 6 (6, 6, 6, 6, 4, 4) rows 4 (4, 3, 3, 3, 1, 1) more time(s), then every 8 (8, 8, 8, 8, 6, 6) rows 6 (6, 7, 7, 7, 12, 12) times—50 (55, 59, 64, 71, 77, 84) sts (see Notes about counting chart sts); piece measures about 12½ (12½, 12¾, 12¾, 12¾, 13, 13)" (31.5 [31.5, 32.5, 32.5, 32.5, 33, 33] cm) from fold line. Work even for 11 rows, beg and ending with a WS row.

INC ROW: (RS) Work in patt to last st, M1, k1— 1 st inc'd.

Cont in patt, rep the inc row every 6 (6, 6, 6, 8, 8, 8) rows 4 (4, 3, 3, 2, 6, 6) more times, then every 8 (8, 8, 8, 10, 0, 0) rows 2 (2, 3, 3, 3, 0, 0) times, working new sts in St st—57 (62, 66, 71, 77, 84, 91) sts. Work even in patt until piece measures 19½ (19½, 20, 20, 20½, 21, 21)" (49.5 [49.5, 51, 51, 52, 53.5, 53.5] cm) from fold line, ending with a RS row.

## Shape Armhole

BO 7 (7, 8, 9, 10, 12, 14) sts at beg of next WS row—50 (55, 58, 62, 67, 72, 77) sts. Dec 1 st at armhole edge (end of RS rows, beg of WS rows) every row 5 (6, 7, 9, 10, 12, 15) times—45 (49, 51, 53, 57, 60, 62) sts rem. Cont in patt until armholes measure 7¾ (7¾, 8, 8¼, 8½, 8¾, 9¼)" (19.5 [19.5, 20.5, 21, 21.5, 22, 23.5] cm), ending with a RS row. Make a note of the last chart row completed so you can work the left front armhole to match.

## Shape Shoulder

BO 6 (7, 8, 8, 10, 10, 11) sts at the beg of the next 2 WS rows, then BO 7 (8, 8, 9, 9, 10, 10) sts at the beg of the next WS row—26 (27, 27, 28, 28, 30, 30) sts rem. Make a note of the last WS chart row completed so you can resume working the patt for the hood with the correct row. Place sts on holder.

# left front

CO 58 (63, 67, 72, 79, 88, 95) sts. Beg with a WS row, work 8 rows in St st, ending with a RS row.

NEXT ROW: (WS) Use the knitted method to CO 3 sts at beg of row, purl across new sts, knit to end for fold line—61 (66, 70, 75, 82, 91, 98) sts.

Working 3 new CO sts at front edge in I-cord edging (see Stitch Guide), work 8 rows in St st, ending with a WS row.

NEXT ROW: (RS) Knit to last 21 sts, pm, work Row 1 of Triple Leaf chart over 15 sts, pm, k3, work 3 edging sts.

Working patts as established, work even until piece measures 4" (10 cm) from fold line, ending with a WS row.

## Shape Waist

DEC ROW: (RS) K1, ssk, work in patt to end—1 st dec'd.

Cont in patt, rep the dec row every 6 (6, 6, 6, 6, 4, 4) rows 4 (4, 3, 3, 3, 1, 1) more time(s), then every 8 (8, 8, 8, 8, 6, 6) rows 6 (6, 7, 7, 7, 12, 12) times—50 (55, 59, 64, 71, 77, 84) sts; piece measures about 12½ (12½, 12¾, 12¾, 12¾, 13, 13)" (31.5 [31.5, 32.5, 32.5, 32.5, 33, 33] cm) from fold line. Work even for 11 rows, beg and ending with a WS row.

INC ROW: (RS) K1, M1, work in patt to end—1 st inc'd.

Cont in patt, rep the inc row every 6 (6, 6, 6, 8, 8, 8) rows 4 (4, 3, 3, 2, 6, 6) more times, then every 8 (8, 8, 8, 10, 0, 0) rows 2 (2, 3, 3, 3, 0, 0) times, working new sts in St st—57 (62, 66, 71, 77, 84, 91) sts. Work even in patt until piece measures 19½ (19½, 20, 20, 20½, 21, 21)" (49.5 [49.5, 51, 51, 52, 53.5, 53.5] cm) from fold line, ending with a WS row.

---

| | knit on RS; purl on WS |
| --- | --- |
| / | k2tog |
| \ | ssk |
| o | yo |
| ⋌ | k3tog |
| ⋋ | k3tog tbl |
| ʌ | sl 2 as if to k2tog, k1, p2sso |
| ▨ | no stitch |

### Triple Leaf

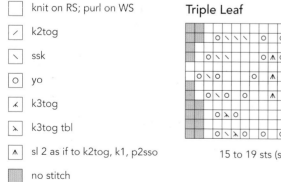

15 to 19 sts (see Notes)

rep for patt

## Shape Armhole

BO 7 (7, 8, 9, 10, 12, 14) sts at beg of next RS row—50 (55, 58, 62, 67, 72, 77) sts. Dec 1 st at armhole edge (beg of RS rows, end of WS rows) every row 5 (6, 7, 9, 10, 12, 15) times—45 (49, 51, 53, 57, 60, 62) sts rem. Cont in patt until armholes measure 7¾ (7¾, 8, 8¼, 8½, 8¾, 9¼)" (19.5 [19.5, 20.5, 21, 21.5, 22, 23.5] cm), ending with the WS row 1 row before the RS chart row that ended the right front armhole.

## Shape Shoulder

BO 6 (7, 8, 8, 10, 10, 11) sts at the beg of the next 2 RS rows, then BO 7 (8, 8, 9, 9, 10, 10) sts at the beg of the next RS row—26 (27, 27, 28, 28, 30, 30) sts rem. Work 1 WS row even to end with the same chart row as the right front. Place sts on holder.

# sleeves

CO 50 (54, 56, 60, 64, 68, 72) sts. Beg with a WS row, work 8 rows in St st, ending with a RS row. Knit 1 WS row for hem fold line. Work in St st until piece measures 3" (7.5 cm) from fold line, ending with a WS row.

INC ROW: (RS) K1, M1, work to last st, M1, k1— 2 sts inc'd.

Cont in St st, rep the inc row every 12 (10, 10, 8, 8, 6, 4) rows 8 (4, 10, 1, 16, 11, 1) more time(s), then every 14 (12, 12, 10, 0, 8, 6) rows 2 (7, 2, 12, 0, 8, 21) times, working new sts in St st—72 (78, 82, 88, 98, 108, 118) sts. Work even in St st until piece measures 18½ (18½, 18½, 19, 19, 19¼, 19¼)" (47 [47, 47, 48.5, 48.5, 49, 49] cm) from fold line, ending with a WS row.

## Shape Sleeve Cap

BO 7 (7, 8, 9, 10, 12, 14) sts at beg of next 2 rows—58 (64, 66, 70, 78, 84, 90) sts rem. Dec 1 st at each side every RS row 2 (3, 4, 5, 5, 6, 5) times, every 4 rows 6 (5, 6, 4, 4, 2, 5) times, every RS row 7 (6, 3, 7, 6, 8, 5) times, then every row 3 (7, 9, 7, 11, 13, 15) times—22 (22, 22, 24, 26, 26, 30) sts rem. BO 3 sts at the beg of the next 2 rows—16 (16, 16, 18, 20, 20, 24) sts. BO all sts.

# finishing

Fold lower body and sleeve hems to WS along fold lines and sew invisibly in place using yarn threaded on a tapestry needle. Block pieces to measurements.

## Hood

With yarn threaded on a tapestry needle, sew shoulder seams. With RS facing, place 26 (27, 27, 28, 28, 30, 30) held right front sts on cir needle, place first 23 (24, 24, 25, 25, 27, 27) held back neck sts on needle, pm at center back, place last 23 (24, 24, 25, 25, 27, 27) back neck sts on needle, place 26 (27, 27, 28, 28, 30, 30) left front sts on needle—98 (102, 102, 106, 106, 114, 114) sts. Rejoin yarn with RS facing at right front edge. Cont in established patts, work even for 1" (2.5 cm), ending with a WS row.

INC ROW: (RS) Work in patt to 1 st before center m, M1, k1, slip marker (sl m), k1, M1, work in patt to end—2 sts inc'd.

Cont in patt, rep the inc row every 6 (6, 4, 4, 4, 6, 6) rows 6 (6, 4, 7, 5, 6, 6) more times, then every 8 (8, 6, 6, 6, 8, 8) rows 3 (3, 8, 6, 8, 4, 4) times, working new sts in St st—118 (122, 128, 134, 134, 136, 136) sts. Work 1 WS row even—hood measures about 8¼ (8¼, 8¾, 8¾, 9¼, 9¼, 9¼)" (21 [21, 22, 22, 23.5, 23.5, 23.5] cm).

NEXT ROW: (RS) Work 56 (58, 61, 64, 64, 65, 65) sts in pattern, k2tog, k1, remove center m, place rem 59 (61, 64, 67, 67, 68, 68) sts on a holder—58 (60, 63, 66, 66, 67, 67) right hood sts rem on needle.

### Right hood

NEXT ROW: (WS) Work even.

NEXT ROW: (RS) Work to last 3 sts, k2tog, k1—1 st dec'd.

Cont in patt, rep the shaping of the last 2 rows 8 more times—49 (51, 54, 57, 57, 58, 58) sts rem.

NEXT ROW: (WS) P1, p2tog, work to end—1 st dec'd.

NEXT ROW: (RS) Work to last 3 sts, k2tog, k1—1 st dec'd.

Rep the last 2 rows 5 more times, then work the WS dec row once more—36 (38, 41, 44, 44, 45, 45) sts rem; hood measures about 12 (12, 12½, 12½, 13, 13, 13)" (30.5 [30.5, 31.5, 31.5, 33, 33, 33] cm). BO all sts.

### Left hood

Return 59 (61, 64, 67, 67, 68, 68) held sts to needle and rejoin yarn with RS facing.

NEXT ROW: (RS) K1, ssk, work to end—1 st dec'd.

NEXT ROW: (WS) Work even.

Cont in patt, rep the shaping of the last 2 rows 9 more times—49 (51, 54, 57, 57, 58, 58) sts rem.

NEXT ROW: (RS) K1, ssk, work to end—1 st dec'd.

NEXT ROW: (WS) Work to last 3 sts, ssp (see Techniques), p1—1 st dec'd.

Rep the last 2 rows 5 more times, then work the RS dec row once more—36 (38, 41, 44, 44, 45, 45) sts rem; hood measures about 12 (12, 12½, 12½, 13, 13, 13)" (30.5 [30.5, 31.5, 31.5, 33, 33, 33] cm). BO all sts.

With yarn threaded on a tapestry needle, sew seam at top of hood. Sew sleeves into armholes. Sew sleeve and side seams. Weave in all loose ends. Block seams and hood, if desired.

# sunday HENLEY

## FINISHED SIZE
32¼ (34, 36¼, 40, 44½, 48¼)" (82 [86.5, 92, 101.5, 113, 122.5] cm) bust circumference. Pullover shown measures 32¼" (82 cm).

## YARN
Sportweight (#2 Fine).

**SHOWN HERE:** Quince & Co. *Chickadee* (100% American wool; 181 yd [166 m]/50 g): #124 goldfinch, 6 (6, 7, 8, 9, 9) skeins.

## NEEDLES
**BODY AND SLEEVES**—size U.S. 7 (4.5 mm): 24" (61 cm) circular (cir) needle.

**RIBBING**—size U.S. 6 (4 mm): 24" (61 cm) cir.

*Adjust needle sizes, if necessary, to obtain the correct gauge.*

## NOTIONS
Markers (m); stitch holders; tapestry needle; five ½" (13 mm) buttons; sewing needle and thread to match buttons.

## GAUGE
21 sts and 30 rows/rnds = 4" (10 cm) in patt from Antique Diamond chart on larger needle.

On any given Sunday, you can walk over to your local park and be treated to a musical performance, breakdance demonstration, or wedding. This henley sweater fits right in with the fun. It's been updated with a slightly lower neckline and two tabs at the elbow sleeves. As seen here, the buttons don't always have to be the same color as your sweater. I love the highly textured pattern of the lace, which is worked on every round or row. Practice the pattern on a slightly larger gauge swatch to learn the pattern before you begin the garment.

## stitch guide

### K1, P1 RIB IN ROUNDS
*(worked over an even number of sts)*

ALL RNDS: *K1, p1; rep from *.

Rep this rnd for patt.

### K1, P1 RIB IN ROWS
*(worked over an even number of sts)*

ALL ROWS: *K1, p1; rep from *.

Rep this row for patt.

### K1, P1 RIB IN ROWS
*(worked over an odd number of sts)*

ROW 1: (RS) K1, *p1, k1; rep from *.

ROW 2: (WS) P1, *k1, p1; rep from *.

Rep Rows 1 and 2 for patt.

## notes

⊖ The body is worked in the round to the start of the front placket, then changes to working back and forth in rows beginning and ending at the center front opening. At the armholes, the body is further divided into the fronts and back, which are worked separately in rows to the shoulders. The sleeves are worked back and forth in rows.

⊖ During shaping, if there are not enough stitches to work a decrease with its companion yarnover, or a double decrease with both its yarnovers, work the remaining stitch(es) in stockinette instead.

⊖ When working the Antique Diamond chart in the round, read all chart rows from right to left as RS rounds. When working back and forth in rows, read the odd-numbered chart rows from right to left as RS rows and read the even-numbered chart rows from left to right as WS rows.

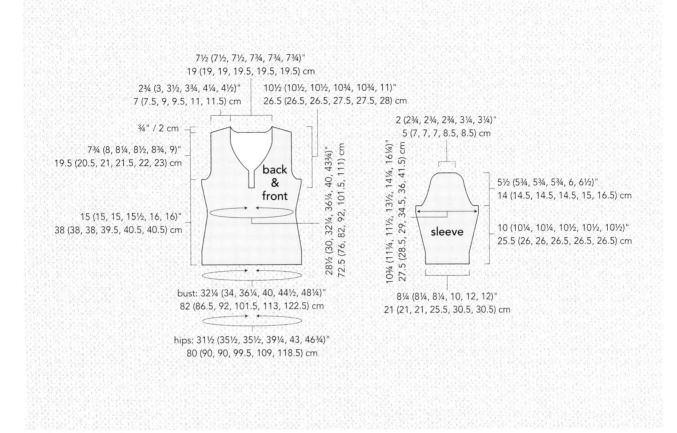

7½ (7½, 7½, 7¾, 7¾, 7¾)"
19 (19, 19, 19.5, 19.5, 19.5) cm

2¾ (3, 3½, 3¾, 4¼, 4½)"
7 (7.5, 9, 9.5, 11, 11.5) cm

10½ (10½, 10½, 10¾, 10¾, 11)"
26.5 (26.5, 26.5, 27.5, 27.5, 28) cm

¾" / 2 cm

7¾ (8, 8¼, 8½, 8¾, 9)"
19.5 (20.5, 21, 21.5, 22, 23) cm

15 (15, 15, 15½, 16, 16)"
38 (38, 38, 39.5, 40.5, 40.5) cm

28½ (30, 32¼, 36¼, 40, 43¾)"
72.5 (76, 82, 92, 101.5, 111) cm

back & front

bust: 32¼ (34, 36¼, 40, 44½, 48¼)"
82 (86.5, 92, 101.5, 113, 122.5) cm

hips: 31½ (35½, 35½, 39¼, 43, 46¾)"
80 (90, 90, 99.5, 109, 118.5) cm

2 (2¾, 2¾, 2¾, 3¼, 3¼)"
5 (7, 7, 7, 8.5, 8.5) cm

10¾ (11¼, 11½, 13½, 14¼, 16¼)"
27.5 (28.5, 29, 34.5, 36, 41.5) cm

5½ (5¾, 5¾, 5¾, 6, 6½)"
14 (14.5, 14.5, 14.5, 15, 16.5) cm

sleeve

10 (10¼, 10¼, 10½, 10½, 10½)"
25.5 (26, 26, 26.5, 26.5, 26.5) cm

8¼ (8¼, 8¼, 10, 12, 12)"
21 (21, 21, 25.5, 30.5, 30.5) cm

# body

With smaller cir needle CO 198 (206, 222, 246, 270, 294) sts. Place marker (pm) and join in the rnd. Work k1, p1 rib in rnds (see Stitch Guide) until piece measures 1½" (3.8 cm). Change to larger cir needle.

NEXT RND: *K3 (6, 3, 3, 3, 4), [k2tog, k4 (8, 4, 4, 4, 4)] 15 (9, 17, 19, 21, 23) times, k2tog, k4 (5, 4, 4, 4, 3),* pm for right side "seam," rep from * to * once more for back—166 (186, 186, 206, 226, 246) sts total; 83 (93, 93, 103, 113, 123) sts each for front and back; rnd begins at left side "seam" at start of front sts.

NEXT RND: *Work Setup Rnd of Antique Diamond chart over 83 (93, 93, 103, 113, 123) sts (see Notes), slip side marker (sl m); rep from * once more.

note: After completing Rnd 8 of the chart, repeat Rows 1–8 for pattern; do not repeat the setup round.

Work in chart patt as established until piece measures 2½" (6.5 cm) from CO.

## Shape Waist

DEC RND: *K1, ssk (see Techniques), work in patt to 3 sts before side m, k2tog, k1, sl m; rep from * once more—4 sts dec'd.

Cont in patt, rep the dec rnd every 12 (6, 12, 12, 12, 12) rnds 3 (6, 3, 3, 1, 1) more time(s), then every 0 (0, 0, 0, 14, 14) rnds 0 (0, 0, 0, 2, 2) times (see Notes)—150 (158, 170, 190, 210, 230) sts rem; 75 (79, 85, 95, 105, 115) sts each for front and back; piece measures 7½ (7½, 7½, 7½, 8, 8)" (19 [19, 19, 19, 20.5, 20.5] cm) from CO. Work even for 9 rnds.

INC RND: *K1, M1 (see Techniques), work to 1 st before side m, M1, k1, sl m; rep from * once more—4 sts inc'd.

Cont in patt, rep the inc rnd every 8 (8, 8, 10, 10, 8) rnds 1 (1, 1, 3, 4, 4) more time(s), then every 10 (10, 10, 0, 0, 0) rnds 2 (2, 2, 0, 0, 0) more times, working new sts into established patt—166 (174, 186, 206, 230, 250) sts total; 83 (87, 93, 103, 115, 125) sts each for front and back. Work even for 3 (5, 7, 8, 0, 8) rnds—piece measures about 13 (13¼, 13½, 14, 14¾, 14¾)" (33 [33.5, 34.5, 35.5, 37.5 37.5] cm) from CO. If the last rnd completed was not an even-numbered chart row, work 1 more rnd.

## Divide for Front Placket

NEXT RND: (odd-numbered chart row) Work 39 (41, 44, 49, 55, 60) left front sts, BO 5 sts at center front, work to end of rnd m—161 (169, 181, 201, 225, 245) sts rem; 39 (41, 44, 49, 55, 60) front sts each side of placket opening, 83 (87, 93, 103, 115, 125) back sts.

Break yarn and rejoin at left front edge with WS facing. Beg working established chart patt back and forth in rows, beg with the next even-numbered WS chart row. Work even if necessary for your size until piece measures 1¼ (1¼, 1,¾,¾,¾)" (3.2 [3.2, 2.5, 2, 2, 2] cm) above last waist inc rnd, ending with a WS row.

NEXT ROW: (RS) *Work in patt to l st before side m, M1, k1, sl m, k1, M1; rep from * once more, work to end—165 (173, 185, 205, 229, 249) sts total; 40 (42, 45, 50, 56, 61) sts each front, 85 (89, 95, 105, 117, 127) back sts.

Work even until piece measures 15 (15, 15, 15½, 16, 16)" (38 [38, 38, 39.5, 40.5, 40.5] cm), ending with a WS row.

## Divide for Fronts and Back

NEXT ROW: (RS) *Work in patt to 5 (5, 5, 6, 8, 10) sts before side seam m, BO 10 (10, 10, 12, 16, 20) sts removing m as you come to it; rep from * once more, work to end—35 (37, 40, 44, 48, 51) sts each front, 75 (79, 85, 93, 101, 107) back sts. Place right front and back sts on separate holders—35 (37, 40, 44, 48, 51) left front sts rem on needle.

# left front

## Shape Armhole

Work 1 WS row even.

Beg on the next RS row, dec 1 st at armhole edge (beg of RS rows, end of WS rows) every row 4 (4, 4, 6, 8, 9) times—31 (33, 36, 38, 40, 42) sts rem. Work even in patt until armhole measures 1 (1½, 1½, 1½, 1¾, 1¾)" (2.5 [3.8, 3.8, 3.8, 4.5, 4.5] cm), ending with a WS row.

## Shape Front Neck

NEXT ROW: (RS) Work in patt to last 3 sts, k2tog, k1—1 st dec'd at neck edge.

Cont in patt, dec 1 st in this manner every RS row 10 (10, 10, 11, 11, 11) more times—20 (22, 25, 26, 28, 30) sts.

NEXT ROW: (WS) P1, p2tog, work in patt to end—1 st dec'd.

NEXT ROW: (RS) Work in patt to last 3 sts, k2tog, k1—1 st dec'd.

**Antique Diamond**

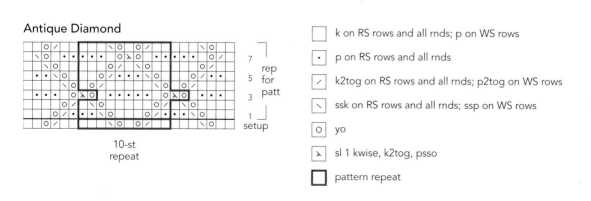

10-st repeat

7
rep
5 for
patt
3
1
setup

☐ k on RS rows and all rnds; p on WS rows

· p on RS rows and all rnds

╱ k2tog on RS rows and all rnds; p2tog on WS rows

╲ ssk on RS rows and all rnds; ssp on WS rows

o yo

⅄ sl 1 kwise, k2tog, psso

☐ pattern repeat

Cont in patt, rep the shaping of the last 2 rows 2 more times—14 (16, 19, 20, 22, 24) sts rem. Cont in patt until armhole measures 7¾ (8, 8¼, 8½, 8¾, 9)" (19.5 [20.5, 21, 21.5, 22, 23] cm), ending with a WS row.

## Shape Shoulder

BO 5 (5, 6, 7, 7, 8) sts at beg of next 2 RS rows, then BO 4 (6, 7, 6, 8, 8) sts at beg of foll RS row—no sts rem.

# right front

Return 35 (37, 40, 44, 48, 51) held right front sts to larger cir needle and rejoin yarn with WS facing. Work 1 WS row even.

## Shape Armhole

Beg on the next RS row, dec 1 st at armhole edge (end of RS rows, beg of WS rows) every row 4 (4, 4, 6, 8, 9) times—31 (33, 36, 38, 40, 42) sts rem. Work even in patt until armhole measures 1 (1½, 1½, 1½, 1¾, 1¾)" (2.5 [3.8, 3.8, 3.8, 4.5, 4.5] cm), ending with a WS row.

## Shape Front Neck

NEXT ROW: (RS) K1, ssk, work in patt to end—1 st dec'd at neck edge.

Cont in patt, dec 1 st in this manner every RS row 10 (10, 10, 11, 11, 11) more times—20 (22, 25, 26, 28, 30) sts.

NEXT ROW: (WS) Work in patt to last 3 sts, ssp (see Techniques), p1—1 st dec'd.

NEXT ROW: (RS) K1, ssk, work in patt to end—1 st dec'd.

Cont in patt, rep the shaping of the last 2 rows 2 more times—14 (16, 19, 20, 22, 24) sts rem. Cont in patt until armhole measures 7¾ (8, 8¼, 8½, 8¾, 9)" (19.5 [20.5, 21, 21.5, 22, 23] cm), ending with a RS row.

## Shape Shoulder

BO 5 (5, 6, 7, 7, 8) sts at beg of next 2 WS rows, then BO 4 (6, 7, 6, 8, 8) sts at beg of foll WS row—no sts rem.

# back

Return 75 (79, 85, 93, 101, 107) held back sts to larger cir needle and rejoin yarn with WS facing. Work 1 WS row even.

## Shape Armhole

Beg on the next RS row, dec 1 st at each side every row 4 (4, 4, 6, 8, 9) times—67 (71, 77, 81, 85, 89) sts rem. Work even in patt until armholes measure 7¾ (8, 8¼, 8½, 8¾, 9)" (19.5 [20.5, 21, 21.5, 22, 23] cm), ending with a WS row.

## Shape Back Neck and Shoulders

NEXT ROW: (RS) BO 5 (5, 6, 7, 7, 8) sts, work in patt until there are 11 (13, 15, 15, 17, 18) sts on right needle after BO, place rem 51 (53, 56, 59, 61, 63) sts on holder—11 (13, 15, 15, 17, 18) right back shoulder sts rem on needle.

### Right shoulder

**NEXT ROW:** (WS) P2tog at neck edge, work to end—10 (12, 14, 14, 16, 17) sts.

**NEXT ROW:** (RS) BO 5 (5, 6, 7, 7, 8) sts, work to last 2 sts, k2tog—4 (6, 7, 6, 8, 8) sts.

**NEXT ROW:** Work even.

BO rem sts.

### Left shoulder

Return 51 (53, 56, 59, 61, 63) held sts to larger cir needle with RS facing and rejoin yarn.

**NEXT ROW:** (RS) BO 35 (35, 35, 37, 37, 37) back neck sts, work to end—16 (18, 21, 22, 24, 26) sts.

**NEXT ROW:** (WS) BO 5 (5, 6, 7, 7, 8) sts, work to last 2 sts, ssp at neck edge—10 (12, 14, 14, 16, 17) sts.

**NEXT ROW:** Ssk, work to end—9 (11, 13, 13, 15, 16) sts.

**NEXT ROW:** BO 5 (5, 6, 7, 7, 8) sts, work to end—4 (6, 7, 6, 8, 8) sts.

**NEXT ROW:** Work even.

BO rem sts.

## sleeves

With smaller cir needle, CO 50 (52, 54, 56, 65, 67) sts. Work k1, p1 rib in rows (see Stitch Guide) until piece measures 1" (2.5 cm), ending with a WS row. Change to larger cir needle.

**NEXT ROW:** (RS) K6 (5, 1, 12, 20, 16), [k2tog, k4 (3, 3, 13, 20, 9)] 6 (8, 10, 2, 1, 3) time(s), k2tog, k6 (5, 1, 12, 21, 16)—43 (43, 43, 53, 63, 63) sts.

**NEXT ROW:** (WS) Work the Setup Row of the Antique Diamond chart as a WS row over all sts.

**note:** *After completing Row 8 of the chart, repeat Rows 1–8 for pattern; do not repeat the setup row.*

Cont in patt from chart until piece measures 2" (5 cm) from CO, ending with a WS row.

**INC ROW:** (RS) K1, M1, work to last st, M1, k1—2 sts inc'd.

Cont in patt, rep the inc row every 8 (6, 6, 6, 10, 4) rows 6 (3, 7, 6, 4, 4) times, then every 0 (8, 8, 8, 12, 6) rows 0 (4, 1, 2, 1, 6) time(s), working new sts into established patt—57 (59, 61, 71, 75, 85) sts. Work even in patt until sleeve measures 10 (10¼, 10¼, 10½, 10½, 10½)" (25.5 [26, 26, 26.5, 26.5, 26.5] cm) from CO, ending with a WS row.

### Shape Sleeve Cap

BO 5 (5, 5, 6, 8, 10) sts at beg of next 2 rows—47 (49, 51, 59, 59, 65) sts rem. Dec 1 st at each side every 4 rows 5 (7, 6, 5, 5, 5) times, then every RS row 8 (5, 7, 6, 8, 9) times, then every row 2 (2, 2, 8, 5, 7) times—17 (21, 21, 21, 23, 23) sts rem. BO 3 sts at beginning of the next 2 rows—11 (15, 15, 15, 17, 17) sts. BO all sts.

# finishing

Block pieces to measurements. With yarn threaded on a tapestry needle, sew shoulder seams. Sew sleeve seams. Sew sleeves into armholes.

## Neckband

With smaller cir needle and RS facing, beg at base of placket opening, pick up and knit 15 sts along right side of placket to start of neck shaping, 45 (45, 45, 47, 47, 47) sts along right neck, 37 (37, 37, 39, 39, 39) sts across back neck, 45 (45, 45, 47, 47, 47) sts along left neck to start of neck shaping, and 15 sts along left side of placket to base of opening—157 (157, 157, 163, 163, 163) sts. Do not join. Work k1, p1 rib for 3 rows, beg and ending with a WS row.

BUTTONHOLE ROW: (RS) Work 5 sts, [yo, k2tog, work 4 sts] 2 times, yo, k2tog work to end—3 buttonholes completed.

Cont in patt for 3 more rows, ending with a WS row. BO all sts in patt with RS facing. Place lower edge of right front band rib on top of left front band rib and sew to sweater. Using sewing needle and thread, sew three buttons to left front band, opposite buttonholes as shown.

## Sleeve Tabs

With smaller cir needle, CO 7 sts. Work in k1, p1 rib for 3½" (9 cm). BO all sts in rib patt. Make a second tab the same as the first. Sew the end of each tab in the center of the WS of the sleeve, with the end of the tab even with the last sleeve cuff rib row. Fold each tab the outside of the sleeve as shown. Using sewing needle and thread, sew a button centered on the end of each tab, sewing through both the tab and sleeve layers.

Weave in all loose ends.

# carriage house
## CARDIGAN

### FINISHED SIZE
32 (36, 40, 44, 48)" (81.5 [91.5, 101.5, 112, 122] cm) bust circumference. Cardigan shown measures 32" (81.5 cm).

**note:** *Bust measurement is determined by doubling the back width.*

### YARN
Laceweight (#0 Lace).

**SHOWN HERE:** Madelinetosh *Tosh Lace* (100% superwash merino wool; 950 yd [869 m]/4 oz [114 g]): filigree, 2 (2, 2, 3, 3) skeins.

### NEEDLES
**BODY AND SLEEVES**—size U.S. 7 (4.5 mm): 24" (61 cm) circular (cir) needle.

**EDGES**—size U.S. 5 (3.75 mm): 24" (61 cm) cir needle.

**TIES**—size U.S. 5 (3.75mm): set of 2 double-pointed needles (dpn).

*Adjust needle sizes, if necessary, to obtain the correct gauge.*

### NOTIONS
Markers (m); removable markers or waste yarn; stitch holders; cable needle (cn); tapestry needle; size D/3 (3.25 mm) crochet hook; safety pin.

### GAUGE
23 sts and 28 rows = 4" (10 cm) in St st on larger needle.

**note:** *This project is deliberately worked at a looser gauge than is typical for laceweight yarn to create an open, drapey effect.*

I am obsessed with laceweight yarns knit on larger needles, the way some little girls are obsessed with horses. You can satisfy both these urges by visiting the tucked-away carriage houses of New York (Yes, they exist! Really!) and knitting this lovely cardigan. The beautiful drape and sheer fabric result in a sweater with a cinched back detail that doesn't feel or look too bulky. When choosing a size for this sweater, go by the measurement across the back on the schematic. Since the fronts are longer and meant to hang open, circumference doesn't really work here.

# back

With smaller cir needle, CO 92 (103, 115, 127, 138) sts. Work in garter stitch (knit all sts every row) until piece measures ½" (1.3 cm). Change to larger cir needle. Work in St st until piece measures 16 (16, 16½, 17, 17)" (40.5 [40.5, 42, 43, 43] cm) from CO. Mark each end of last row completed with removable markers or waste yarn to indicate base of armholes. Work even in St st for 6¾ (7¼, 7½, 8¼, 9)" (17 [18.5, 19, 21, 23] cm) more, or desired length to shoulders, ending with a WS row—piece measures 22¾ (23¼, 24, 25¼, 26)" (58 [59, 61, 64, 66] cm) from CO.

## Shape Back Neck and Shoulders

BO 5 (6, 8, 8, 9) sts at the beginning of the next 4 rows—72 (79, 83, 95, 102) sts.

**NEXT ROW:** (RS) BO 5 (6, 7, 8, 9), knit until there are 13 (14, 15, 18, 21) sts on right needle after BO, place rem 54 (59, 61, 69, 72) sts on holder—13 (14, 15, 18, 21) right back shoulder sts rem on needle.

### Right shoulder

**NEXT ROW:** (WS) P2tog at neck edge, work to end—12 (13, 14, 17, 20) sts.

**NEXT ROW:** (RS) BO 5 (6, 7, 8, 9) sts, work to last 2 sts, k2tog—6 (6, 6, 8, 10) sts.

**NEXT ROW:** Work even.

BO rem sts.

### Left shoulder

Return 54 (59, 61, 69, 72) held sts to larger cir needle with RS facing and rejoin yarn.

**NEXT ROW:** (RS) BO 36 (39, 39, 43, 42) back neck sts, work to end—18 (20, 22, 26, 30) sts.

**NEXT ROW:** (WS) BO 5 (6, 7, 8, 9) sts, work to last 2 sts, ssp (see Techniques) at neck edge—12 (13, 14, 17, 20) sts.

**NEXT ROW:** Ssk, work to end—11 (12, 13, 16, 19) sts.

**NEXT ROW:** BO 5 (6, 7, 8, 9) sts, work to end—6 (6, 6, 8, 10) sts.

**NEXT ROW:** Work even.

BO rem sts.

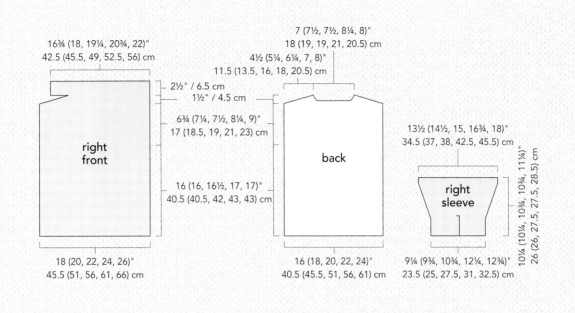

16¾ (18, 19¼, 20¾, 22)"
42.5 (45.5, 49, 52.5, 56) cm

7 (7½, 7½, 8¼, 8)"
18 (19, 19, 21, 20.5) cm

4½ (5¼, 6¼, 7, 8)"
11.5 (13.5, 16, 18, 20.5) cm

2½" / 6.5 cm
1½" / 4.5 cm

6¾ (7¼, 7½, 8¼, 9)"
17 (18.5, 19, 21, 23) cm

13½ (14½, 15, 16¾, 18)"
34.5 (37, 38, 42.5, 45.5) cm

**right front**

**back**

**right sleeve**

16 (16, 16½, 17, 17)"
40.5 (40.5, 42, 43, 43) cm

10¼ (10¼, 10¾, 10¾, 11¼)"
26 (26, 27.5, 27.5, 28.5) cm

18 (20, 22, 24, 26)"
45.5 (51, 56, 61, 66) cm

16 (18, 20, 22, 24)"
40.5 (45.5, 51, 56, 61) cm

9¼ (9¾, 10¾, 12¼, 12¾)"
23.5 (25, 27.5, 31, 32.5) cm

# right front

With smaller cir needle, CO 104 (115, 127, 138, 150) sts. Work in garter stitch until piece measures ½" (1.3 cm). Change to larger cir needle.

**NEXT ROW:** (RS) Knit.

**NEXT ROW:** (WS) Purl to last 5 sts, k5 for front edge.

Rep the last 2 rows until piece measures 16 (16, 16½, 17, 17)" (40.5 [40.5, 42, 43, 43] cm) from CO. Mark the side edge (end of RS rows, beg of WS rows) of last row completed with removable marker or waste yarn to indicate base of armhole. Cont in St st with 5 front edge sts in garter st for 6¾ (7¼, 7½, 8¼, 9)" (17 [18.5, 19, 21, 23] cm) more, or same length as back, ending with a RS row—piece measures 22¾ (23¼, 24, 25¼, 26)" (58 [59, 61, 64, 66] cm) from CO.

## Shape Shoulder

Cont front edge sts as established, BO 5 (6, 8, 8, 9) sts at beg of next 2 WS rows, then 5 (6, 7, 8, 9) sts at beg of foll 2 WS rows, then 6 (6, 6, 8, 10) sts at beg of next WS row—78 (85, 91, 98, 104) sts.

**NEXT ROW:** (RS) Knit to end, then use the backward-loop method (see Techniques) to CO 18 (19, 19, 22, 22) sts at end of row for back neck extension—96 (104, 110, 120, 126) sts.

Cont front edge sts as established, work until neck extension measures 2" (5 cm) from new CO sts, ending with a RS row. Change to smaller cir needle, work all sts in garter stitch for 5 rows—piece measures 2½" (6.5 cm) from new CO sts. Change to larger cir needle and BO all sts loosely.

# left front

With smaller cir needle, CO 104 (115, 127, 138, 150) sts. Work in garter stitch until piece measures ½" (1.3 cm). Change to larger cir needle.

**NEXT ROW:** (RS) Knit.

**NEXT ROW:** (WS) K5 for front edge, purl to end.

Rep the last 2 rows until piece measures 16 (16, 16½, 17, 17)" (40.5 [40.5, 42, 43, 43] cm) from CO. Mark the side edge (beg of RS rows, end of WS rows) of last row completed with removable

marker or waste yarn to indicate base of armhole. Cont in St st with 5 front edge sts in garter st for 6¾ (7¼, 7½, 8¼, 9)" (17.5 [18.5, 19, 21, 23] cm) more, or same length as back, ending with a WS row—piece measures 22¾ (23¼, 24, 25¼, 26)" (58 [59, 61, 64, 66] cm) from CO.

## Shape Shoulder

Cont front edge sts as established, BO 5 (6, 8, 8, 9) sts at beg of next 2 RS rows, then 5 (6, 7, 8, 9) sts at beg of foll 2 RS rows, then 6 (6, 6, 8, 10) sts at beg of next RS row—78 (85, 91, 98, 104) sts.

NEXT ROW: (WS) K5, purl to end, then use the backward-loop method to CO 18 (19, 19, 22, 22) sts at end of row for back neck extension—96 (104, 110, 120, 126) sts.

Cont front edge sts as established, work until neck extension measures 2" (5 cm) from new CO sts, ending with a RS row. Change to smaller cir needle, work all sts in garter stitch for 5 rows—piece measures 2½" (6.5 cm) from new CO sts. Change to larger cir needle and BO all sts loosely.

# right sleeve

note: *The lower sleeve is worked in two halves to create a center slit, then joined for working in one piece to the end.*

With smaller cir needle, CO 29 (30, 33, 37, 39) sts. Work in garter stitch (knit all sts every row) until piece measures ½" (1.3 cm). Change to larger cir needle and work in St st until piece measures 2½" (6.5 cm) from CO, ending with a WS row. Break yarn, place sts on holder, and set aside. Work a second piece in the same manner and leave sts on needle. With RS facing, return 29 (30, 33, 37, 39) held sts to end of needle so the group of sts with the working yarn attached will be worked first on the next RS row.

JOINING ROW: (RS) Knit to last 4 sts of first half, place next 4 sts on cn and hold in back, *insert right needle tip into first st on left needle then into first st on cn and work them together as k2tog; rep from * 3 more times, knit to end of second half—54 (56, 62, 70, 74) sts.

Work 3 rows even in St st, ending with a WS row—piece measures 3" (7.5 cm) from CO.

INC ROW: (RS) K1, M1 (see Techniques), knit to last st, M1, k1—2 sts inc'd.

Cont in St st, rep the inc row every 4 (2, 4, 4, 2) rows 11 (3, 9, 12, 3) more times, then every 0 (4, 6, 0, 4) rows 0 (10, 2, 0, 11) times, working new sts in St st—78 (84, 86, 96, 104) sts. Work even until sleeve measures 10¼ (10¼, 10¾, 10¾, 11¼)" (26, 26, 27.5, 27.5, 28.5] cm) from CO. BO all sts loosely.

## left sleeve

Work as right sleeve to joining row—2 groups of sts on needle with 29 (30, 33, 37, 39) sts each.

**JOINING ROW:** (RS) Knit to last 4 sts of first half, place next 4 sts on cn and hold in front, *insert right needle tip into first st on cn then into first st on left needle and work them together as k2tog; rep from * 3 more times, knit to end of second half—54 (56, 62, 70, 74) sts.

Complete as for right sleeve.

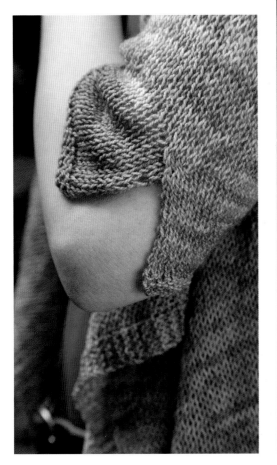

# finishing

Block pieces to measurements. Using yarn and crochet hook, join shoulders using the slip-stitch crochet seam method (see Techniques). With yarn threaded on a tapestry needle, sew short ends of back neck extensions together, then sew selvedge of neck extension along back neck. Sew tops of sleeves to body between armhole markers and sew sleeve and side seams also using the slip-stitch crochet seam method.

## Back Cinch

With dpn, CO 4 sts. Work I-cord (see Techniques) until piece measures 60" (152.5 cm) long for drawstring. BO all sts. With larger cir needle, CO 12 sts for drawstring casing. Work in St st until piece measures 14" (35.5 cm) long. BO all sts. Lay sweater flat with WS of back facing up. Pin casing to center of WS of back with WS of pieces touching, the casing oriented vertically (the long sides run up and down), and the bottom short end of the casing even with the first St st row above the garter st lower edge. With yarn threaded on a tapestry needle, sew around the two long sides and short top edge of casing, leaving the bottom open. Sew a line down the middle of the casing through both layers of fabric, starting about ¾" (2 cm) below the top of the casing. Secure the safety pin on one end of the drawstring, and starting at the bottom opening, thread the drawstring up one half of the casing, across the top, and back down the other side to emerge at the bottom opening again. Pull the ends of the drawstring even, cinch the lower back as shown in the photographs, and tie in a bow.

Weave in all loose ends.

# secret garden
## TANK

### FINISHED SIZE
31½ (34, 37, 40½, 44)" (80 [86.5, 94, 103, 112] cm) bust circumference. Tank shown measures 31½" (80 cm).

### YARN
Sportweight (#2 Fine) and Laceweight (#0 Lace).

**SHOWN HERE:** Louet *Euroflax Sport Weight* (100% wet-spun linen; 270 yd [246 m]/ 100 g): #67 seafoam green (MC), 3 (3, 3, 4, 4) skeins.

Filatura Di Crosa *Nirvana* (100% extrafine merino wool; 372 yd [340 m]/25 g): #11 natural (CC), 1 ball for all sizes.

### NEEDLES
**BODY**—size U.S. 4 (3.5 mm): 24" (61 cm) circular (cir) needle.

**EDGING**—size U.S. 3 (3.25 mm): 24" (61 cm) cir needle.

*Adjust needle sizes, if necessary, to obtain the correct gauge.*

### NOTIONS
Markers (m); stitch holders; tapestry needle; four ½" (13 mm) buttons; sewing needle and thread to match buttons.

### GAUGE
23 sts and 28 rows = 4" (10 cm) in St st using MC on larger needle.

Linen is such an interesting fiber, and, in my opinion, it does not get enough street cred. On first look, it's easy to pass over on the yarn-shop shelf as being too stiff and scratchy, because its real beauty doesn't reveal itself until it's been washed and lovingly roughed up a bit. The fabric only improves with time, and it's the perfect fiber for warmer summer months. This tank uses linen's natural drape to its advantage, and its slightly swingy shape features a surprise lace insert in the back.

## stitch guide

### SIMPLE EYELET
*(multiple of 8 sts)*

ROWS 1 AND 5: (RS) Knit.

ROWS 2, 4, AND 6: (WS) Purl.

ROW 3: *K6, yo, ssk; rep from * to end.

ROW 7: K2, *yo, ssk, k6; rep from * to last 6 sts, yo, ssk, k4.

ROW 8: Purl.

Rep Rows 1–8 for patt.

## notes

⊖ Linen is beautiful, but it does tend to grow a bit lengthwise when worn. An easy solution to this problem is to choose a size with some negative ease, 1" to 2" (2.5–5 cm) less than your bust measurement should do the trick. When the garment is stretched widthwise, it doesn't have as much extra to give in the length department.

⊖ The lace panel is worked separately and sewn into the lower back opening during finishing.

⊖ The stitch count of the Lace Border chart does not remain constant throughout. It begins with 10 stitches, increases to 13 stitches after completing Row 1, then decreases back to 10 stitches after completing Row 12.

⊖ For Row 2 of the Lace Border chart, work the first 3 stitches as yo, p2tog, k1, then work [k1, p1] twice into the large loop formed by the quadruple yarnover from Row 1, and work the rest of the row as shown on the chart.

⊖ For Row 12 for the Lace Border chart, bind off the first 3 stitches, then return the stitch on the right needle after the last bind-off to the left needle, and work the rest of the row as yo, p2tog, k5, p1, k2 as shown on the chart.

## back

### Right Lower Back

With MC and smaller cir needle, CO 38 (42, 46, 51, 56) sts. Work in garter st (knit all sts every row) until piece measures ½" (1.3 cm). Change to larger cir needle.

NEXT ROW: (RS) Knit.

NEXT ROW: (WS) K3, purl to end.

Rep the last 2 rows until piece measures 4" (10 cm) from CO, ending with a WS row.

INC ROW: (RS) Knit to last 4 sts, M1 (see Techniques), k4—1 st inc'd.

Cont as established with 3 edge sts in garter st, rep the inc row every 16 (18, 18, 18, 18) rows 2 more times—41 (45, 49, 54, 59) sts. Work even until piece measures 9½ (10, 10, 10, 10)" (24 [25.5, 25.5, 25.5, 25.5] cm) from CO, ending with a RS row. Place sts on holder.

### Left Lower Back

With MC and smaller cir needle, CO 38 (42, 46, 51, 56) sts. Work in garter st (knit all sts every row) until piece measures ½" (1.3 cm). Change to larger cir needle.

NEXT ROW: (RS) Knit.

NEXT ROW: (WS) Purl to last 3 sts, k3.

Rep the last 2 rows until piece measures 4" (10 cm) from CO, ending with a WS row.

INC ROW: (RS) K4, M1, knit to end—1 st inc'd.

Cont as established with 3 edge sts in garter st, rep the inc row every 16 (18, 18, 18, 18) rows 2 more times—41 (45, 49, 54, 59) sts. Work even until piece measures 9½ (10, 10, 10, 10)" (24 [25.5, 25.5, 25.5, 25.5] cm) from CO, ending with a RS row. Leave sts on needle.

### Join Right and Left Back

Turn work so WS is facing. Return 41 (45, 49, 54, 59) held right lower back sts to end of needle so left lower back sts with the working yarn attached will be worked first on the next WS row.

JOINING ROW: (WS) Purl to last 3 sts of left lower back, k3; work first 3 sts of right lower back as k3, purl to end—82 (90, 98, 108, 118) sts.

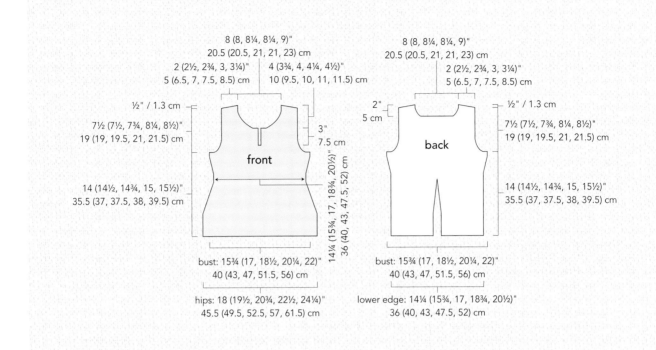

Front diagram measurements:
- 8 (8, 8¼, 8¼, 9)" / 20.5 (20.5, 21, 21, 23) cm
- 2 (2½, 2¾, 3, 3¼)" / 5 (6.5, 7, 7.5, 8.5) cm
- 4 (3¾, 4, 4¼, 4½)" / 10 (9.5, 10, 11, 11.5) cm
- ½" / 1.3 cm
- 7½ (7½, 7¾, 8¼, 8½)" / 19 (19, 19.5, 21, 21.5) cm
- 3" / 7.5 cm
- front
- 14 (14½, 14¾, 15, 15½)" / 35.5 (37, 37.5, 38, 39.5) cm
- 14¼ (15¾, 17, 18¾, 20½)" / 36 (40, 43, 47.5, 52) cm
- bust: 15¾ (17, 18½, 20¼, 22)" / 40 (43, 47, 51.5, 56) cm
- hips: 18 (19½, 20¾, 22½, 24¼)" / 45.5 (49.5, 52.5, 57, 61.5) cm

Back diagram measurements:
- 8 (8, 8¼, 8¼, 9)" / 20.5 (20.5, 21, 21, 23) cm
- 2 (2½, 2¾, 3, 3¼)" / 5 (6.5, 7, 7.5, 8.5) cm
- 2" / 5 cm
- ½" / 1.3 cm
- 7½ (7½, 7¾, 8¼, 8½)" / 19 (19, 19.5, 21, 21.5) cm
- back
- 14 (14½, 14¾, 15, 15½)" / 35.5 (37, 37.5, 38, 39.5) cm
- bust: 15¾ (17, 18½, 20¼, 22)" / 40 (43, 47, 51.5, 56) cm
- lower edge: 14¼ (15¾, 17, 18¾, 20½)" / 36 (40, 43, 47.5, 52) cm

## Upper Back

NEXT ROW: (RS) Knit.

NEXT ROW: (WS) Purl to 6 garter sts in center, k6, purl to end.

Change to working all sts in St st. Work even until piece measures 10½ (11, 11, 11, 11)" (26.5 [28, 28, 28, 28] cm) from CO, ending with a WS row.

## Shape Bust

INC ROW: (RS) K1, M1, knit to last st, M1, k1—2 sts inc'd.

Cont in St st, rep the inc row every 4 rows 3 more times—90 (98, 106, 116, 126) sts. Work even until piece measures 14 (14½, 14¾, 15, 15½)" (35.5 [37, 37.5, 38, 39.5] cm) from CO, ending with a WS row.

## Shape Armholes

BO 6 (6, 7, 8, 9) sts at beg of next 2 rows—78 (86, 92, 100, 108) sts.

NEXT ROW: (RS) K4, ssk (see Techniques), knit to last 6 sts, k2tog, k4—2 sts dec'd.

NEXT ROW: (WS) K4, p2tog, purl to last 6 sts, ssp (see Techniques), k4—2 sts dec'd.

Rep last 2 rows 1 (2, 2, 3, 3) more time(s), then work the RS dec row 1 (0, 0, 1, 1) more time(s)—68 (74, 80, 82, 90) sts rem. Keeping 4 sts at each side in garter st, work in St st until armholes measure 6 (6, 6¼, 6¾, 7)" (15 [15, 16, 17, 18] cm), ending with a WS row.

## Shape Back Neck and Shoulders

NEXT ROW: (RS) Work 13 (16, 18, 19, 21) sts for right back shoulder, place rem 55 (58, 62, 63, 69) sts on holder.

### Right shoulder

NEXT ROW: (WS) P2tog at neck edge, purl to last 4 sts, k4—12 (15, 17, 18, 20) sts.

NEXT ROW: (RS) Knit to last 2 sts, k2tog—11 (14, 16, 17, 19) sts.

Keeping 4 sts at armhole edge in garter st, work

even as established until armhole measures 7½ (7½, 7¾, 8¼, 8½)" (19 [19, 19.5, 21, 21.5] cm), ending with a WS row. BO 6 (7, 8, 9, 10) sts at beg of next RS row—5 (7, 8, 8, 9) sts rem. Work 1 WS row even. BO all sts.

## Left shoulder

Return 55 (58, 62, 63, 69) held sts to larger cir needle with RS facing and rejoin yarn.

**NEXT ROW:** (RS) BO 42 (42, 44, 44, 48) back neck sts, work to end—13 (16, 18, 19, 21) sts.

**NEXT ROW:** (WS) K4, purl to last 2 sts, ssp at neck edge—12 (15, 17, 18, 20) sts.

**NEXT ROW:** Ssk, knit to end—11 (14, 16, 17, 19) sts.

Keeping 4 sts at armhole edge in garter st, work even as established until armhole measures 7½ (7½, 7¾, 8¼, 8½)" (19 [19, 19.5, 21, 21.5] cm), ending with a RS row. BO 6 (7, 8, 9, 10) sts at beg of next WS row—5 (7, 8, 8, 9) sts rem. Work 1 RS row even. BO all sts.

# front

With MC and smaller cir needle, CO 104 (112, 120, 130, 140) sts. Work in garter st until piece measures ½" (1.3 cm). Change to larger cir needle. Work even in St st until piece measures 4" (10 cm) from CO, ending with a WS row.

## Shape Waist

Place dart markers and begin princess-style shaping on next row as foll:

**NEXT ROW:** (RS) K26 (28, 30, 32, 35), place marker (pm), k2tog, k48 (52, 56, 62, 66), ssk, pm, k26 (28, 30, 32, 35)—102 (110, 118, 128, 138) sts.

**NEXT ROW:** (WS) Purl.

**DEC ROW:** Knit to first dart m, slip marker (sl m), k2tog, knit to 2 sts before next dart m, ssk, sl m, knit to end—2 sts dec'd.

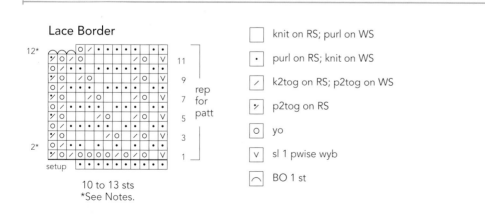

### Lace Border

12*

11

9

rep
for
patt

7

5

3

2*

1

setup

10 to 13 sts
*See Notes.

| | knit on RS; purl on WS |
| --- | --- |
| • | purl on RS; knit on WS |
| ╱ | k2tog on RS; p2tog on WS |
| ⅄ | p2tog on RS |
| O | yo |
| V | sl 1 pwise wyb |
| ⌒ | BO 1 st |

Cont in St st, rep the dec row every 4 rows 9 more times—82 (90, 98, 108, 118) sts; piece measures about 9½" (24 cm) from CO for all sizes. Work even until piece measures 10½ (11, 11, 11, 11)" (26.5 [28, 28, 28, 28] cm) from CO, ending with a WS row.

INC ROW: (RS) Work to first dart m, sl m, M1, knit to next dart m, M1, sl m, knit to end—2 sts inc'd.

Cont in St st, rep the inc row every 4 rows 3 more times—90 (98, 106, 116, 126) sts. Removing the dart markers on the next row, work even until piece measures 14 (14½, 14¾, 15, 15½)" (35.5 [37, 37.5, 38, 39.5] cm) from CO, ending with a WS row.

## Shape Armholes

BO 6 (6, 7, 8, 9) sts at beg of next 2 rows—78 (86, 92, 100, 108) sts.

NEXT ROW: (RS) K4, ssk, knit to last 6 sts, k2tog, k4—2 sts dec'd.

NEXT ROW: (WS) K4, p2tog, purl to last 6 sts, ssp, k4—2 sts dec'd.

Rep last 2 rows 1 (2, 2, 3, 3) more time(s), then work the RS dec row 1 (0, 0, 1, 1) more time(s)—68 (74, 80, 82, 90) sts rem. Keeping 4 sts at each side in garter st, work in St st if necessary for your size until armholes measure 1 (1¼, 1¼, 1½, 1½)" (2.5 [3.2, 3.2, 3.8, 3.8] cm), ending with a WS row.

## Shape Front Neck

NEXT ROW: (RS) K32 (35, 38, 39, 43) for left front, place rem 36 (39, 42, 43, 47) sts on holder.

### Left neck and shoulder

Keeping 4 sts at armhole edge in garter st, work even on 32 (35, 38, 39, 43) left neck sts until armhole measures 4 (4¼, 4¼, 4½, 4½)" (10 [11, 11, 11.5, 11.5] cm), ending with a RS row.

NEXT ROW: (WS) BO 5 (5, 6, 6, 7) sts, purl to last 4 sts, k4—27 (30, 32, 33, 36) sts.

Dec 1 st at neck edge (end of RS rows, beg of WS rows) every row 16 (16, 16, 16, 17) times—11 (14, 16, 17, 19) sts. Work even until armhole measures 7½ (7½, 7¾, 8¼, 8½)" (19 [19, 19.5, 21, 21.5] cm), ending with a WS row. BO 6 (7, 8, 9, 10) sts at beg of next RS row—5 (7, 8, 8, 9) sts rem. Work 1 WS row even. BO all sts.

### Right neck and shoulder

Return 36 (39, 42, 43, 47) held sts to larger cir needle with RS facing and rejoin yarn.

**NEXT ROW:** (RS) BO 4 sts, knit to end—32 (35, 38, 39, 43) sts.

Keeping 4 sts at armhole edge in garter st, work even on right neck sts until armhole measures 4 (4¼, 4¼, 4½, 4½)" (10 [11, 11, 11.5, 11.5] cm), ending with a WS row.

**NEXT ROW:** (RS) BO 5 (5, 6, 6, 7) sts, knit to end—27 (30, 32, 33, 36) sts.

Dec 1 st at neck edge (beg of RS rows, end of WS rows) every row 16 (16, 16, 16, 17) times—11 (14, 16, 17, 19) sts. Work even until armhole measures 7½ (7½, 7¾, 8¼, 8½)" (19 [19, 19.5, 21, 21.5] cm), ending with a RS row. BO 6 (7, 8, 9, 10) sts at beg of next WS row—5 (7, 8, 8, 9) sts rem. Work 1 RS row even. BO all sts.

# finishing

Block pieces to measurements. With yarn threaded on a tapestry needle, sew shoulder seams. Sew side seams.

## Buttonband

Using MC and smaller cir needle, with RS facing and beg at neck edge, pick up and knit 17 sts along straight section of left front neck. Work in garter st for 4 rows, ending with a RS row. With WS facing, BO all sts kwise.

## Buttonhole Band

Using MC and smaller cir needle, with RS facing and beg at lower right corner of neck opening, pick up and knit 17 sts along straight section of right front neck. Knit 1 WS row.

**BUTTONHOLE ROW:** (RS) K3, *work a 2-st one-row buttonhole (see Techniques), knit until there are 2 sts on right needle after buttonhole; rep from * once more, work a 2-st one-row buttonhole, knit to end—3 buttonholes completed; the 4th buttonhole will be worked in the neckband later.

Knit 2 rows, ending with a RS row. With WS facing, BO all sts kwise.

## Neckband

With MC and smaller cir needle, with RS facing and beg at BO edge of buttonhole band, pick up and knit 102 (102, 108, 116, 120) sts evenly around neck opening, ending at BO edge of button band. Knit 3 rows, ending with a WS row.

**BUTTONHOLE ROW:** (RS) K2, work a 2-st one-row buttonhole, knit to end—4th buttonhole completed.

Knit 1 WS row. With WS facing, BO all sts kwise.

## Lace Insert

With CC and larger cir needle, CO 10 sts. Work the setup row of Lace Border chart once, then rep Rows 1–12 of chart 5 (5, 5, 6, 6) times (do not rep the setup row; see Notes)—61 (61, 61, 73, 73) rows total. BO all sts. Hold border with RS facing and straight selvedge running across the top. With CC and larger cir needle, pick up and knit 32 (32, 32, 40, 40) sts along straight selvedge. Purl 1 WS row. Work in Simple Eyelet patt (see Stitch Guide) until piece measures 9½ (10, 10, 10, 10)" (24 [25.5, 25.5, 25.5, 25.5] cm) along side edges (it will measure slightly longer at the tips of the border points), ending with a WS row.

**NEXT ROW:** (RS) *K2tog; rep from * to end—16 (16, 16, 20, 20) sts.

**NEXT ROW:** (WS) Purl.

**NEXT ROW:** *K2tog; rep from * to end—8 (8, 8, 10, 10) sts.

BO all sts.

Block insert to about 7½ (7½, 7½, 9, 9)" (19 [19, 19, 23, 23] cm) wide across the border at the bottom, and 9½ (10, 10, 10, 10)" (24 [25.5, 25.5, 25.5, 25.5] cm) tall, taking care not to flatten the gathers at the top. With MC threaded on a tapestry needle, sew insert into opening at center back as shown, overlapping the back opening's garter border on top of the insert at each side and across the top, and sewing in the "ditch" between the garter border and St st fabric.

Weave in all loose ends. Using sewing needle and thread, sew buttons to left front, opposite buttonholes.

# grand army plaza

## SHAWL

### FINISHED SIZE
About 54" (137 cm) across top edge and 24" (61 cm) long from center of top edge to lower point, blocked.

### YARN
Laceweight (#0 Lace).

**SHOWN HERE:** Sundara Yarn *Silk Lace* (100% silk; 1000 yd [914 m]/100 g): island breeze, 1 skein.

### NEEDLES
Size U.S. 4 (3.5 mm): 24" (61 cm) cir needle and one double-pointed needle (dpn).

*Adjust needle size, if necessary, to obtain the correct gauge; exact gauge is not critical for this project.*

### NOTIONS
Tapestry needle; rustproof blocking pins.

### GAUGE
16 sts and 24 rows = 4" (10 cm) in average gauge of lace patts, after blocking.

Years ago, I knit a full circular shawl that I love and wear all the time. It's very pretty and impressive laid out flat in its full glory, but you only get half the effect when it's worn.

Enter the half-circle shawl! You can wear this the same way you would a triangle or full circle, but all your knitting will be seen and appreciated. As an added bonus, the garter-based lace patterns used here are mostly reversible, and the fabric doesn't curl.

This shawl evokes the tucked-away niches of green that you can find anywhere in New York.

# stitch guide

## ROMAN STRIPE
### (worked on an even number of patt sts + 4 edge sts)

ROW 1: K2 (edge sts), *yo, k1; rep from * to last 2 sts, k2 (edge sts)—sts have inc'd to twice the original patt sts, plus 2 edge sts at each side.

ROW 2: K2, purl to last 2 sts, k2.

ROW 3: K2, *k2tog; rep from * to last 2 sts, k2—sts have dec'd to original number.

ROWS 4 AND 5: K2, *yo, k2tog; rep from to last 2 sts, k2.

ROWS 6 AND 7: Knit.

Rep Rows 1–7 for patt.

## MADEIRA MESH
### (multiple of 6 sts + 7)

ROWS 1–6: K2, *yo, p3tog, yo, k3; rep from *, to last 5 sts, yo, p3tog, yo, k2.

ROWS 7–12: K2, *k3, yo, p3tog, yo; rep from * to last 5 sts, k5.

Rep Rows 1–12 for patt.

## DOUBLE FAGGOTING
### (multiple of 4 sts + 1)

ROW 1: (RS) K3, *yo, p3tog, yo, k1; rep from * to last 2 sts, k2.

ROW 2: (WS) K2, p2tog, yo, k1, *yo, p3tog, yo, k1; rep from * last 4 sts, yo, p2tog, k2.

Rep Rows 1 and 2 for patt.

# notes

⊖ The shawl begins in the center of the upper edge and is worked downward with increases to shape the half circle.

⊖ The lace edging is worked perpendicularly to the body of the shawl, joining one edging stitch together with one live shawl stitch at the end of every even-numbered edging row until all the shawl stitches have been consumed.

# shawl

CO 8 sts.

ROW 1: Knit.

ROW 2: K2, *yo, k1; rep from * to last 2 sts, k2—12 sts.

ROWS 3–5: Knit.

ROW 6: K2, *yo, k1; rep from * to last 2 sts, k2—20 sts.

ROWS 7–12: Knit.

ROW 13: K2, *yo, k1; rep from * to last 2 sts, k2—36 sts.

ROWS 14–25: Knit.

ROW 26: K2, *yo, k1; rep from * to last 2 sts, k2—68 sts.

ROWS 27–28: Knit.

ROWS 29–49: Work Rows 1–7 of Roman Stripe patt (see Stitch Guide) 3 times.

ROWS 50–51: Knit.

ROW 52: K2, *yo, k1; rep from * to last 2 sts, k2—132 sts.

ROWS 53–58: Knit.

ROW 59: K2, M1 (see Techniques), knit to end—133 sts.

ROWS 60–101: Work Rows 1–12 of Madeira Mesh patt (see Stitch Guide) 3 times, then work Rows 1–6 once more.

ROW 102: K2, *yo, k1; rep from * to last 3 sts, k3—261 sts.

ROWS 103–142: Work Rows 1 and 2 of Double Fagoting patt (see Stitch Guide) 20 times.

ROWS 143–145: Knit.

## Lace Edging

Turn the work so the end of the cir needle with working yarn is in your right hand. Use the backward-loop method (see Techniques) to CO 10 sts onto the end of the right needle—271 sts total; 261 live shawl sts, 10 edging sts. Turn the work so the end of the cir needle with the new CO sts is in your left hand and use the dpn instead of the other cir needle tip to work the edging as foll:

**SETUP ROW:** K9, k2tog (last edging st tog with shawl st after it), turn work—10 edging sts; 1 shawl st joined.

**ROW 1:** K2, yo, k2tog, k2, k2tog, yo, k2.

**ROW 2:** K3, yo, k2, yo, k4, k2tog (last edging st tog with next shawl st), turn work—12 edging sts; 1 shawl st joined.

**ROW 3:** K2, yo, k10—13 edging sts.

**ROW 4:** BO 3 sts (1 st rem on right needle after last BO), k8, k2tog (last edging st tog with next shawl st), turn work—10 edging sts; 1 shawl st joined.

Rep Rows 1–4 (do not rep the setup row) 129 more times—10 edging sts rem; all shawl sts have been joined. BO rem sts.

# finishing

Weave in all loose ends. Soak shawl in a basin of water. To block, pin the top edge along a straight line to about 54" (137 cm) wide. Pin the center point straight down from the middle of the top edging to measure about 24" (61 cm) long, then pin out the rem points on each side of center, forming a half-circle shape.

# courtyard
## PULLOVER

**FINISHED SIZE**

30½ (33¼, 35¼, 37¼, 40, 42, 45½)" (77.5 [84.5, 89.5, 94.5, 101.5, 106.5, 115.5] cm) bust circumference. Pullover shown measures 33¼" (84.5 cm).

**YARN**

DK Weight (#3 Light).

**SHOWN HERE:** Fleece Artist *Woolie Silk 3 ply* (65% wool, 35% silk; 252 yd [230 m]/ 100 g): smoke, 4 (5, 5, 5, 6, 6, 7) skeins.

**NEEDLES**

**BODY AND SLEEVES**—size U.S. 6 (4 mm): 24" (61 cm) circular (cir) needle and double-pointed needle (dpn).

**RIBBING**—size U.S. 4 (3.5 mm) 24" (61 cm) cir needle and dpn.

*Adjust needle sizes, if necessary, to obtain the correct gauge.*

**NOTIONS**

Markers (m); waste yarn for holders; tapestry needle.

**GAUGE**

20 sts and 28 rows/rnds = 4" (10 cm) in St st on larger needles.

20 sts and 32½ rnds = 4" (10 cm) in texture stripe patt on larger needles.

When I designed this pullover, I had in mind an easy, no-fuss garment that goes with everything, that you never want to take off, and that's suitable for anything from a casual courtyard party to a restaurant brunch with family. To jazz it up, I added a mix of different knitting patterns together to form an interesting textured stripe. If you get carried away with the rhythm of knitting around and around, since the pattern is uneven, don't worry if you mix up a round or two. Sometimes it's just nice to enjoy the process.

# stitch guide

## K1, P1, RIB
### (worked on an even number of sts)

ALL RNDS: *K1, p1; rep from * to end.

Rep this rnd for patt.

## TEXTURE STRIPE

RNDS 1–4: Knit.

RND 5: *K2tog, yo; rep from *, ending k1 if there is an odd number of sts.

RNDS 6 AND 7: Knit.

RND 8: Purl.

RND 9: *K1, yo; rep from *, ending k1 if there is an odd number of sts.

RND 10: *P1, drop yo from needle; rep from *, ending p1 if there is an odd number of sts; the dropped yarnovers will create a rnd of elongated sts.

RNDS 11–17: Knit.

RND 18: Purl.

RND 19: Knit.

RND 20: Purl.

RND 21: *K2tog, yo; rep from *, ending k1 if there is an odd number of sts.

RNDS 22–32: Knit.

RND 33: Purl.

RND 34: Knit.

RND 35: Purl.

RND 36: *Ssk, yo, k2, yo, k2tog, k1; rep from *, ending as foll:

If 1 (2) st(s) rem, end k1 (2).

If 3 (4) sts rem, end ssk, yo, k1 (2).

If 5 sts rem, end ssk, yo, k3.

If 6 sts rem, end ssk, yo, k2, yo, k2tog.

RND 37: Knit.

RNDS 38–40: Rep Rnds 36 and 37, then work Rnd 36 once more.

RND 41: Purl.

RND 42: Knit.

RND 43: Purl.

RNDS 44–48: Knit.

RND 49: *K2tog, yo; rep from * to end, ending k1 if there is an odd number of sts.

RNDS 50–52: Knit.

RND 53: Purl.

RNDS 54–56: Knit.

RND 57: Purl.

Rep Rnds 1–57 for patt.

# notes

- This project is worked in the round from the top down.

- The yoke will be divided into sections (back, front, and sleeves) by the raglan increases, so it will not be possible to work the texture stripe pattern continuously around the yoke. Begin the pattern at the start of the round, work to the end of each section, then resume the pattern where you left off as well as possible at the start of the next section.

- At the beginning and end of the yoke sections, as well as during waist and sleeve shaping, if there are not enough stitches to work a decrease with its companion yarnover, work the remaining stitch in stockinette instead.

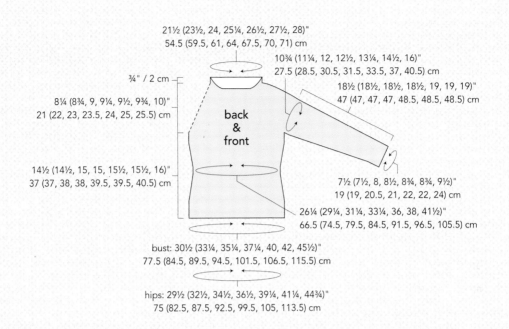

21½ (23½, 24, 25¼, 26½, 27½, 28)"
54.5 (59.5, 61, 64, 67.5, 70, 71) cm

10¾ (11¼, 12, 12½, 13¼, 14½, 16)"
27.5 (28.5, 30.5, 31.5, 33.5, 37, 40.5) cm

18½ (18½, 18½, 18½, 19, 19, 19)"
47 (47, 47, 47, 48.5, 48.5, 48.5) cm

¾" / 2 cm

8¼ (8¾, 9, 9¼, 9½, 9¾, 10)"
21 (22, 23, 23.5, 24, 25, 25.5) cm

back & front

14½ (14½, 15, 15, 15½, 15½, 16)"
37 (37, 38, 38, 39.5, 39.5, 40.5) cm

7½ (7½, 8, 8½, 8¾, 8¾, 9½)"
19 (19, 20.5, 21, 22, 22, 24) cm

26¼ (29¼, 31¼, 33¼, 36, 38, 41½)"
66.5 (74.5, 79.5, 84.5, 91.5, 96.5, 105.5) cm

bust: 30½ (33¼, 35¼, 37¼, 40, 42, 45½)"
77.5 (84.5, 89.5, 94.5, 101.5, 106.5, 115.5) cm

hips: 29½ (32½, 34½, 36½, 39¼, 41¼, 44¾)"
75 (82.5, 87.5, 92.5, 99.5, 105, 113.5) cm

# yoke

## Neckband

With larger cir needle, *CO 38 (43, 44, 47, 50, 51, 52) sts, place marker (pm), CO 16 (16, 16, 16, 16, 18, 18) sts, pm; rep from * once more, join in the rnd—108 (118, 120, 126, 132, 138, 140) sts total; rnd begins at left back raglan, at start of back sts.

Work in St st for 5 rnds. Change to smaller cir needle and work k1, p1 rib (see Stitch Guide) for 3 rnds—piece measures about ¾" (2 cm) with lower edge allowed to roll.

## Shape Back Neck

Change to larger cir needle. Work St st back and forth in short rows (see Techniques) as foll:

SHORT ROW 1: (RS) Knit across (38 (43, 44, 47, 50, 51, 52) back sts, slip marker (sl m), knit across 16 (16, 16, 16, 16, 18, 18) right sleeve sts, sl m, k8 (11, 11, 13, 13, 15, 15) front sts, wrap next st, turn.

SHORT ROW 2: (WS) Purl to end of front, sl m, purl across right sleeve sts, sl m, purl across back sts, sl m, purl across left sleeve sts, sl m, p8 (11, 11, 13, 13, 15, 15) front sts, wrap next st, turn.

SHORT ROWS 3 AND 4: Work to 10 (12, 12, 13, 13, 14, 14) sts before previous wrapped st, wrap next st, turn.

SHORT ROWS 5 AND 6: Work to 11 (12, 12, 13, 13, 15, 15) sts before previous wrapped st, wrap next st, turn.

SHORT ROWS 7 AND 8: Work to 11 (12, 12, 13, 14, 15, 15) sts before previous wrapped st, wrap next st, turn.

With RS facing, knit to end-of-rnd m, working wraps tog with wrapped sts as you come to them. Knit 1 more rnd, working rem wrapped st—piece measures 1½" (3.8 cm) from end of neckband rib at center back; no change to length at center front.

## Shape Raglans

Change to texture stripe patt (see Stitch Guide and Notes), and work yoke shaping as foll:

**INC RND:** *K1, M1 (see Techniques), work in patt to 1 st before next m, M1, k1, sl m; rep from * 3 more times—8 sts inc'd; 2 sts each for back, front, and both sleeves.

**note:** *Keep 1 stitch on each side of all four raglan markers in stockinette as you work the following yoke shaping.*

Cont in patt, rep the inc rnd every 4 (4, 4, 4, 2, 2, 2) rnds 12 (13, 15, 14, 2, 1, 8) more time(s), then every 6 (6, 0, 6, 4, 4, 4) rnds 1 (1, 0, 1, 15, 16, 13) time(s), working new sts into texture stripe patt (see Notes)—220 (238, 248, 254, 276, 282, 316) sts; 66 (73, 76, 79, 86, 87, 96) sts each for back and front, 44 (46, 48, 48, 52, 54, 62) sts each sleeve—piece measures about 8¼ (8¾, 9, 9¼, 9½, 9¾, 10)" (21 [22, 23, 23.5, 24, 25, 25.5] cm) from end of neckband rib at center back and 1½" (3.8 cm) shorter at center front. If necessary, cont in patt until you end with a knit rnd that will be followed by another knit rnd.

## Divide for Body and Sleeves

**DIVIDING RND:** *Knit to sleeve m, remove m, place next 44 (46, 48, 48, 52, 54, 62) sleeve sts on waste yarn holder, remove second sleeve m, use the backward-loop method to CO 5 (5, 6, 7, 7, 9, 9) underarm sts, pm for side "seam," CO 5 (5, 6, 7, 7, 9, 9) more underarm sts; rep from * once more—152 (166, 176, 186, 200, 210, 228) sts; 76 (83, 88, 93, 100, 105, 114) sts each for back and front. Make a note of the patt rnd just completed so you can resume working the sleeves with the correct rnd later.

# body

**NEXT RND:** *Work in patt to 1 st before side m, p1, sl m; rep from * once more.

**note:** *As you work the following instructions, continue to purl the "seam" stitch before each side marker every round until the ribbing at the end of the body.*

Work even in patt until piece measures 1¾" (4.5 cm) from dividing rnd.

## Shape Waist

**DEC RND:** *Ssk (see Techniques), work to 3 sts before m, k2tog, p1, sl m; rep from * once more—4 sts dec'd, 2 sts each from back and front.

Cont in patt, rep the dec rnd every 6 (6, 8, 8, 8, 8, 8) rnds 2 (2, 3, 3, 3, 3, 2) more times, then every 8 (8, 10, 10, 10, 10, 10) rnds 2 (2, 1, 1, 1, 1, 2) time(s)—132 (146, 156, 166, 180, 190, 208) sts rem; 66 (73, 78, 83, 90, 95, 104) sts each for back and front; piece measures 5¼ (5¼, 6, 6, 6, 6, 6¼)" (13.5 [13.5, 15, 15, 15, 15, 16] cm) from dividing rnd. Work even for 10 rnds.

**INC RND:** *M1, work to 1 st before side m, M1, p1, sl m; rep from * once more—4 sts inc'd, 2 sts each for back and front.

Cont in patt, rep the inc rnd every 12 (12, 12, 12, 14, 14, 14) rnds 2 (2, 2, 2, 3, 3, 2) more times, then every 14 (14, 14, 14, 0, 0, 16) rnds 1 (1, 1, 1, 0, 0, 1) time(s), working new sts into patt—148 (162, 172, 182, 196, 206, 224) sts; 74 (81, 86, 91, 98, 103, 112) sts each for front and back.

Work even until piece measures 13¾ (13¾, 14¼, 14¼, 14¾, 14¾, 15¼)" (35 [35, 36, 36, 37.5, 37.5, 38.5] cm) from dividing rnd, ending with a knit rnd of the patt.

Change to smaller cir needle. Work 3 rnds in k1, p1 rib. Change to larger cir needle. Knit 5 rnds. BO all sts loosely—piece measures about 14½ (14½, 15, 15, 15½, 15½, 16)" (37 [37, 38, 38, 39.5, 39.5, 40.5] cm) from dividing rnd with lower edge allowed to roll.

## sleeves

With larger dpn, CO 5 (5, 6, 7, 7, 9, 9) sts for first half of underarm, work 44 (46, 48, 48, 52, 54, 62) held sleeve sts in established patt, CO 5 (5, 6, 7, 7, 9, 9) sts for second half of underarm—54 (56, 60, 62, 66, 72, 80) sts. Pm and join in the rnd. Work in patt for 1" (2.5 cm).

**DEC RND:** Ssk, work to last 2 sts, k2tog—2 sts dec'd.

Cont in patt, rep the dec rnd every 16 (14, 12, 12, 12, 8, 8) rnds 3 (4, 3, 3, 8, 3, 13) more times, then every 18 (16, 14, 14, 14, 10, 10) rnds 4 (4, 6, 6, 2, 10, 2) times—38 (38, 40, 42, 44, 44, 48) sts.

Work even until sleeve measures 17¾ (17¾, 17¾, 17¾, 18¼, 18¼, 18¼)" (45 [45, 45, 45, 46.5, 46.5, 46.5] cm) from dividing rnd, ending with a knit rnd of the patt. Change to smaller dpn. Work 3 rnds in k1, p1 rib. Change to larger dpn. Knit 5 rnds. BO all sts loosely—sleeve measures about 18½ (18½, 18½, 18½, 19, 19, 19)" (47 [47, 47, 47, 48.5, 48.5, 48.5] cm) from dividing rnd with lower edge allowed to roll.

## finishing

Block to measurements. With yarn threaded on a tapestry needle, sew underarm seams. Weave in all loose ends.

# seams

## Crochet Seam

Make a slipknot and place it on a crochet hook. *Insert hook through both pieces of fabric one stitch in from selvedge (Figure 1), wrap yarn around hook to make a loop, pull this loop back through the fabric and through loop already on the hook (Figure 2). Repeat from *.

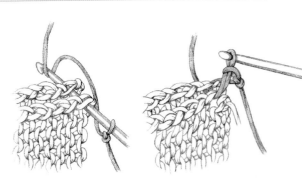

figure 1          figure 2

## Mattress Stitch with 1-stitch Seam Allowance

Place the pieces to be seamed on a table, right sides facing up. Begin at the lower edge and work upward.

Insert threaded needle under one bar between the two edge stitches on one piece, then under the corresponding bar plus the bar above it on the other piece (Figure 1). *Pick up the next two bars on the first piece (Figure 2), then the next two bars on the other (Figure 3). Repeat from *, ending by picking up the last bar or pair of bars on the first piece.

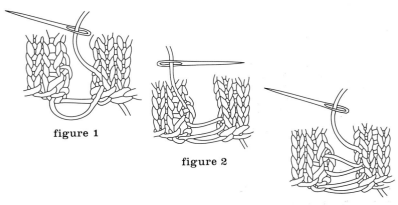

figure 1

figure 2

figure 3

# buttonholes

## One-row Buttonhole

For a 3 (4, 5)-st buttonhole. Work to where you want the buttonhole to begin, bring the yarn to the front, slip the next stitch purlwise, and then return the yarn to the back.

*Slip the next stitch. Then on the right needle, pass the second stitch over the end stitch (Figure 1). Repeat from * 2 (3, 4) times. Slip the last bound-off stitch to the left needle and turn the work.

Move the yarn to the back and use the cable cast-on to cast on 4 (5, 6) stitches as follows: *Insert the right needle between the first and second stitches on the left needle, draw up a loop, and place it on the left needle (Figure 2). Repeat from * 3 (4, 5) times. Turn the work.

With the yarn in back, slip the first stitch from the left needle and pass the extra cast-on stitch over it to close the buttonhole (Figure 3). Continue as instructed.

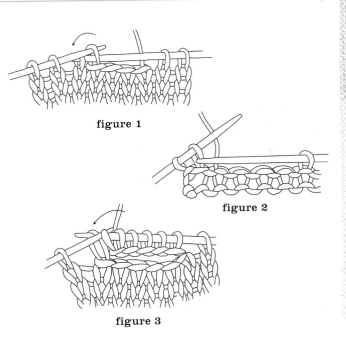

figure 1

figure 2

figure 3

# grafting

## Kitchener Stitch

Arrange stitches on two needles so that there is the same number of stitches on each needle. Hold the needles parallel to each other with wrong sides of the knitting together. Allowing about ½" (1.3 cm) per stitch to be grafted, thread matching yarn on a tapestry needle. Work from right to left as follows:

**STEP 1.** Bring tapestry needle through the first stitch on the front needle as if to purl and leave the stitch on the needle (**Figure 1**).

**STEP 2.** Bring tapestry needle through the first stitch on the back needle as if to knit and leave that stitch on the needle (**Figure 2**).

**STEP 3.** Bring tapestry needle through the first front stitch as if to knit and slip this stitch off the needle, then bring tapestry needle through the next front stitch as if to purl and leave this stitch on the needle (**Figure 3**).

**STEP 4.** Bring tapestry needle through the first back stitch as if to purl and slip this stitch off the needle, then bring tapestry needle through the next back stitch as if to knit and leave this stitch on the needle (**Figure 4**).

Repeat Steps 3 and 4 until one stitch remains on each needle, adjusting the tension to match the rest of the knitting as you go. To finish, bring tapestry needle through the front stitch as if to knit and slip this stitch off the needle, then bring tapestry needle through the back stitch as if to purl and slip this stitch off the needle.

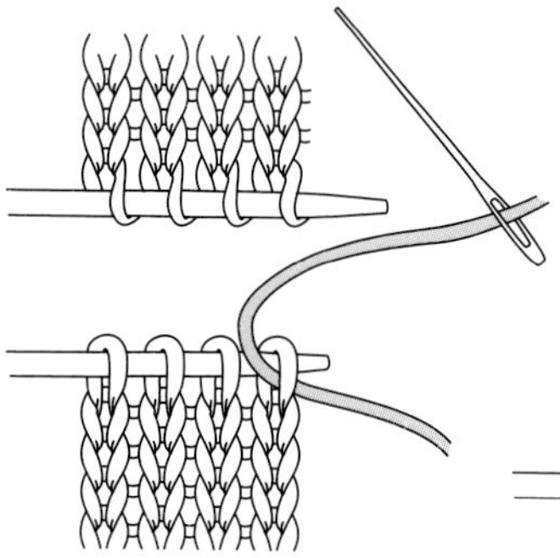

figure 1

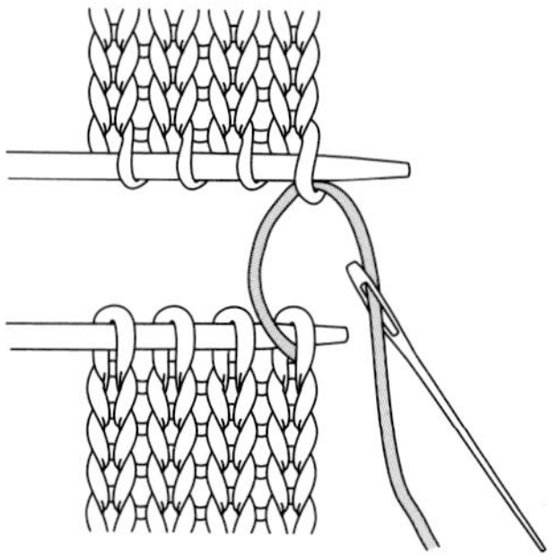

figure 2

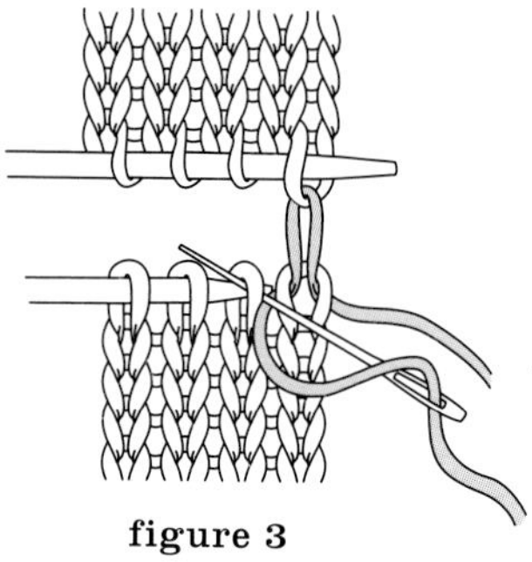

figure 3

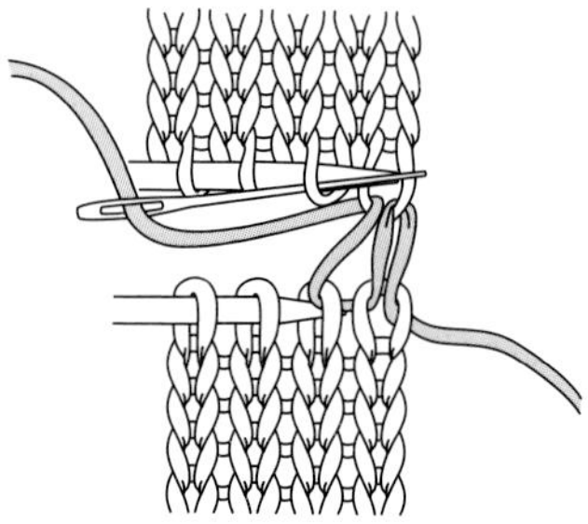

figure 4

# pick up and knit

## Along CO or BO Edge

With right side facing and working from right to left, insert the tip of the needle into the center of the stitch below the bind-off or cast-on edge (**Figure 1**), wrap yarn around needle, and pull through a loop (**Figure 2**). Pick up one stitch for every existing stitch.

## Along Shaped Edge

With right side facing and working from right to left, insert tip of needle between last and second-to-last stitches, wrap yarn around needle, and pull through a loop. Pick up and knit about three stitches for every four rows, adjusting as necessary so that picked-up edge lies flat.

figure 1

figure 2

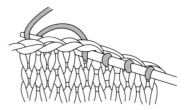

# short-rows

### Knit Side

Work to turning point, slip next stitch purlwise (**Figure 1**), bring the yarn to the front, then slip the same stitch back to the left needle (**Figure 2**), turn the work around and bring the yarn in position for the next stitch—one stitch has been wrapped, and the yarn is correctly positioned to work the next stitch. When you come to a wrapped stitch on a subsequent row, hide the wrap by working it together with the wrapped stitch as follows: Insert right needle tip under the wrap (from the front if wrapped stitch is a knit stitch; from the back if wrapped stitch is a purl stitch; **Figure 3**), then into the stitch on the needle, and work the stitch and its wrap together as a single stitch.

### Purl Side

Work to the turning point, slip the next stitch purlwise to the right needle, bring the yarn to the back of the work (**Figure 1**), return the slipped stitch to the left needle, bring the yarn to the front between the needles (**Figure 2**), and turn the work so that the knit side is facing—one stitch has been wrapped, and the yarn is correctly positioned to knit the next stitch. To hide the wrap on a subsequent purl row, work to the wrapped stitch, use the tip of the right needle to pick up the wrap from the back, place it on the left needle (**Figure 3**), then purl it together with the wrapped stitch.

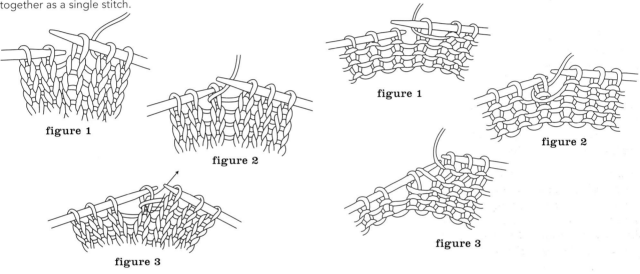

figure 1

figure 2

figure 3

# i-cord (also called knit-cord)

This is worked with two double-pointed needles. Cast on the desired number of stitches (usually three to four). Knit across these stitches, then *without turning the needle, slide stitches to other end of needle, pull the yarn around the back, and knit the stitches as usual. Repeat from * for desired length.

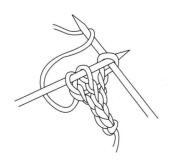

# crochet chain (ch)

Make a slipknot and place it on crochet hook if there isn't a loop already on the hook. *Yarn over hook and draw through loop on hook. Repeat from * for the desired number of stitches. To fasten off, cut yarn and draw end through last loop formed.

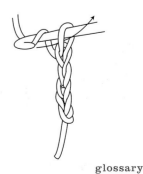

# sources for yarns

**Berroco Inc.**

1 Tupperware Dr., Ste. 4
North Smithfield, RI 02896
berroco.com
*Ultra Alpaca*

**Bijou Basin Ranch**

PO Box 154
Elbert, CO 80106
bijoubasinranch.com
*Lhasa Wilderness*

**Blue Sky Alpacas**

PO Box 88
Cedar, MN 55011
blueskyalpacas.com
*Alpaca Silk*

**Brown Sheep Company Inc.**

100662 County Rd. 16
Mitchell, NE 69357
brownsheep.com
*Lanaloft Sport*

**Cascade Yarns**

PO Box 58168
1224 Andover Pk. E.
Tukwila, WA 98188
cascadeyarns.com
*Ecological Wool*

**The Fibre Company**

Distributed by Kelbourne Woolens
2000 Manor Rd.
Conshohocken, PA 19428
kelbournewoolens.com
*Road to China Light*

**Fleece Artist**

fleeceartist.com
*Woolie Silk 3 ply*

**Frog Tree Yarns**

Distributed by T&C Imports
PO Box 1119
East Dennis, MA 02641
frogtreeyarns.com
*Alpaca Sport*

**Hand Maiden Fine Yarn**

handmaiden.ca
*Mini Maiden*

**Lorna's Laces**

4229 N. Honore St.
Chicago, IL 60613
lornaslaces.net
*Shepherd Sock*

**Louet North America/Gems**

3425 Hands Rd.
Prescott, ON
Canada K0E 1T0
louet.com
*Euroflax*

**Madelinetosh**

7515 Benbrook Pkwy.
Benbrook, TX 76126
madelinetosh.com
*Tosh Lace*

**Malabrigo Yarn**

malabrigoyarn.com
*Merino Worsted*

**Manos del Uruguay**

Distributed by Fairmount Fibers
PO Box 2082
Philadelphia, PA 19103
fairmountfibers.com
*Serena*

**O-Wool**

Distributed by Tunney Wool Company
915 N. 28th St.
Philadelphia, PA 19130
o-wool.com
*Classic Worsted*

**Quince and Company**

quinceandco.com
*Chickadee*

**Rowan**

Distributed in the United States by
Westminster Fibers Inc.
165 Ledge St.
Nashua, NH 03060
westminsterfibers.com
*Kidsilk Haze*

**Sundara Yarn**

PO Box 1118
Carlsborg, WA 98324
sundarayarn.com
*Sundara Lace*

**Tahki-Stacy Charles Inc.**

70–60 83rd St., Bldg. #12
Glendale, NY 11385
tahkistacycharles.com
*Filatura Di Crosa Nirvana*

**Valley Yarns**

Distributed by Webs
75 Service Center Rd.
Northampton, MA 01060
yarn.com
*Amherst*

# index

# Add these new resources

## FROM INTERWEAVE TO YOUR KNITTING LIBRARY

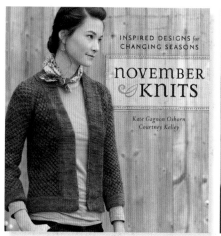

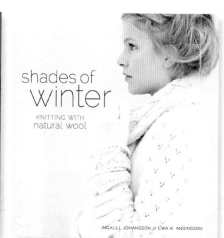

**November Knits**

Inspired Designs for Changing Seasons
Kate Gagnon Osborn and Courtney Kelley
ISBN 978-1-59668-439-3
$24.95

**French Girl Knits Accessories**

Modern Designs for a Beautiful Life
Kristeen Griffin-Grimes
ISBN 978-1-59668-490-4
$21.95

**Shades of Winter**

Knitting with Natural Wool
Ingalill Johansson and Ewa K. Andinsson
ISBN 978-1-59668-786-8
$24.95

shop.knittingdaily.com

*Knitting Daily* is a friendly online community where you'll meet other fiber enthusiasts, learn new techniques and tips from industry experts, meet up-and-coming knitwear designers and celebrity authors, access the latest knitting patterns, and more! **knittingdaily.com**

*Interweave Knits* inspires and informs the modern knitter with projects and articles that celebrate the handmade life. Each issue features lush projects from your favorite designers, in-depth technique articles to further your knitting knowledge, information on the latest must-have yarns, designer profiles, and much more.
**interweaveknits.com**